Limited War Revisited

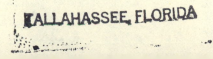

A Westview Special Study

Limited War Revisited
Robert E. Osgood

The strategy of limited war has transformed the American approach to the use of force and played a key role in U.S. foreign policy since World War II. As the mainstay of containment it was designed to deter and fight wars effectively at a tolerable cost and risk in the nuclear age by providing the United States with a flexible and controlled response to a variety of military threats. The strategy met a severe challenge in the Vietnam war; it has nevertheless continued to prevail as a doctrine, if not necessarily with its former utility, by adapting to the changing domestic and international environment after Vietnam.

Robert E. Osgood critically examines the success, ambiguities, and flaws of the strategy in its expanding application to postwar military policy. He interprets its impact on the Vietnam war and vice versa, extends his analysis to the new challenges posed by changes in technology and the military balance that affect U.S. security, and concludes with a searching inquiry into the problems of limited war where its utility as an instrument of foreign policy is now most in doubt: the Third World.

Robert E. Osgood was dean of the School of Advanced International Studies, Johns Hopkins University (1973-1976), where he still is professor of American foreign policy and holds the Christian A. Herter Chair.

Published in Cooperation with
The Johns Hopkins Washington Center
of Foreign Policy Research

Limited War Revisited
Robert E. Osgood

Westview Press / Boulder, Colorado

This is a Westview reprint edition, manufactured on our own premises using equipment and methods that allow us to keep even specialized books in stock. It is printed on acid-free paper and bound in softcovers that carry the highest rating of NASTA in consultation with the AAP and the BMI.

A Westview Special Study

Copyright © 1979 by Westview Press, Inc.

Published in 1979 in the United States of America by
Westview Press, Inc.
5500 Central Avenue
Boulder, Colorado 80301
Frederick A. Praeger, Publisher

Library of Congress Cataloging in Publication Data
Osgood, Robert Endicott.
    Limited war revisited.
    (A Westview special study)
    1. Limited war. 2. United States—Military policy. 3. Military history, Modern—20th century. I. Title.
UA11.5.083   355.02'15   79-13427
ISBN 0-89158-465-X

Printed and bound in the United States of America

10   9   8

To
Virginia Maria

Contents

Foreword

How has the Vietnam war affected the theory and practice of limited war? Now that the emotions aroused by the U.S. involvement in Indochina begin to subside, a resumption of the debate over the circumstances, modalities, and requirements of limited war becomes all the more important in the light of the numerous changes that have helped to transform the international system this past decade. "The search for lessons," Robert E. Osgood writes, "naturally begins with the reasons for failure." Admittedly, the "lessons" presented here are still tentative, but they do represent an initial contribution to a process of historical interpretation that will be pursued for many years to come. As Osgood makes clear, however, the reassessment of limited-war strategy must go far beyond the lessons of Vietnam. To this end, *Limited War Revisited* fits especially well the effort of The Johns Hopkins Washington Center of Foreign Policy Research to reassess the foundations of U.S. foreign policy in a changing international and domestic setting.

We would like to express our profound gratitude to the Lewis and Rosa Strauss Memorial Fund, which helped to underwrite a series of meetings on limited war held at the Center in the spring of 1978. It was for one of those meetings that a first draft of this volume was initially written. We are also indebted to Colin Gray, Geoffrey Kemp, and Fred Iklé, whose papers,

specifically written for that series, made a significant contribution to the further elaboration of Professor Osgood's essay;
to Paul H. Nitze who chaired so diligently and so construc-
tively all our meetings; and to the many participants in our
seminars whose comments proved to be especially useful and
constructive.

Simon Serfaty
Director, Washington Center of
Foreign Policy Research

Abbreviations

ARVN	Armed forces of (South) Vietnam
C³	Communications, command, and control system
GVN	Government of South Vietnam
ICBM	Intercontinental ballistic missile
IRBM	Intermediate range ballistic missile
MBFR	Mutual balanced force reductions
MC 14/3	NATO's official strategic posture statement, December 1967
MIRV	Multiple independently targeted reentry vehicle
MPLA	Marxist Peoples Liberation Alliance
MRBM	Medium range ballistic missile
NATO	North Atlantic Treaty Organization
NSAM	National Security Action Memorandum
NVA	North Vietnamese Army
OPEC	Organization of Petroleum Exporting Countries
PGM	Precision guided munitions
SALT	Strategic arms limitation talks
TNW	Tactical nuclear weapons
VC	Vietcong cadres
WP	Warsaw Pact

Limited War Revisited

1
Limited War
in U.S. Foreign Policy

The Historical Context

All military strategies reflect the national values and foreign policies they are supposed to protect. The history of the U.S. strategy of limited war is central to the history of U.S. foreign policy since the end of World War II. An examination of the current state of limited-war strategy against the background of its inception, ascendance, elaboration, crisis, and reassessment is, therefore, an inquiry about the state of U.S. foreign policy as well. But the U.S. strategy of limited war also has an important place in the general history of international politics. As a doctrine for the times, and as an aspect of U.S. foreign policy, it has affected and will continue to affect the issues of war and peace. This reassessment of the postwar strategy of limited war therefore begins with the broad historical setting from which the strategy emerged and ends with the current trends in U.S. foreign policy from which its future character and impact will largely arise.

Limited wars are as old as the history of mankind, as ubiquitous as armed conflict. In the history of international conflict the wars that have been truly momentous and rare are those that were fought to annihilate, to completely defeat or completely dominate the adversary. These wars have been the principal stimulus of theories and doctrines of how to limit and fight wars as rational instruments of national policy.

In modern times the consciousness of limited war as a distinct kind of armed conflict, to be understood and practiced according to special theories and doctrines, has emerged in reaction to the growing capacity and inclination of states to wage general, total warfare. In the eighteenth century a theory and doctrine of limited war—tactical, legal, and political—developed in reaction to the devastation of the Wars of Religion. In the nineteenth century, when military thought and policies were dominated by the prophets of blitzkrieg and wars of annihilation, Karl von Clausewitz reacted against the wars of the French Revolution and Napoleon; he stands out as the preeminent military and political strategist of limited war in modern times. In the twentieth century the resurgence of limited-war theory, strategy, and tactics is rooted in the widespread revulsion to two world wars. But the detailed elaboration of strategies of limited war and the prominent role these strategies have played in international politics and military policies since World War II are derived particularly from the fear of nuclear destruction and the exigencies of the cold war.

Actually there have been two strands to the resurgence of limited-war theories and doctrines since World War II, reflecting two different political perspectives in the cold war. One strand, inspired by the concepts of Clausewitz and propounded by Western political scientists and defense specialists, has sought to make force, in both war and deterrence, an effective instrument of containment against the Soviet Union, China, and the international Communist parties aligned with them. The other strand, inspired by Mao Tse-tung and Third-World nationalism and propounded by revolutionary nationalists, has sought to use guerrilla warfare to abolish Western colonialism and hegemony and establish new nations ostensibly dedicated to social justice.[1]

The first strand of theory looks to deliberate restraint and the measured use of force to deter or defeat Communist military expansion without running an unacceptable risk of general war. The second strand envisions the use of limited means—the strategy of insurgency—to achieve total political conquest. This essay is concerned primarily with the former and only secondarily with the latter when it becomes a concern of the former.

The postwar theory of limited war raised the question of how to distinguish limited from general or total war. The theory was developed specifically as an alternative to a third world war, which, in the nuclear age, was believed to be as disastrous for the victor as for the vanquished, and as a counter to the Western (preeminently U.S.) concept of war as the use of maximum force to overwhelm the enemy and compel his unconditional surrender. The anti-Western theory of insurgency, in contrast, implicitly limited war by the methods and traditions of revolutionary war. There was no need to define or dwell upon the process of *limitation*—only the need to expound the strategy and tactics of *winning* a national revolutionary war.

The generally accepted definition of limited war that emerged in the West in the 1950s limited both the means and ends of war. Limited wars were to be fought for ends far short of the complete subordination of one state's will to another's, using means that involve far less than the total military resources of the belligerents and leave the civilian life and the armed forces of the belligerents largely intact. According to a strict application of this definition, limited war is not only a matter of degree but also a matter of national perspective—a local war that is limited from the standpoint of external participants might be total from the standpoint of the local belligerents, as in the Korean and Vietnam wars. Clearly, the Western definition of limited war, like the theory, reflected not some universal reality but the interests of the Western allies, especially of the United States, in a particular period of international conflict.

In this period—the cold war through Vietnam—international conflict was punctuated by numerous local limited wars. Most of them were "internal wars"—dozens of insurrections and rebellions and a number of larger-scale civil wars within the boundaries of a state or between the two parts of a divided state but usually with foreign support.[2] Although these internal wars

arose essentially from indigenous conflict, many of them were
viewed as contests between Communist and anti-Communist
forces—as in Greece, 1946-1949; China, 1946-1950; Indochina,
1947-1954; Malaya, 1948-1958; the Philippines, 1949-1955;
Korea, 1950-1953; Guatemala, 1954; Algeria, 1954-1962;
Cuba, 1957-1959; Lebanon, 1959; the Congo, 1960-1963;
the Dominican Republic, 1965; and Vietnam, 1959-1975—
and most of them were simultaneously supported by the
superpowers and their allies. On the other hand, relatively few
local wars, discounting a great number of border clashes, were
direct armed encounters between undivided states—notably,
the Suez war of 1956, the Arab-Israeli wars of 1948-1949,
1967, and 1973; the India-Pakistan wars of 1965 and 1971;
and the India-China border war of 1959-1962. Except for the
India-China conflict, these wars were not fought between
Communist and anti-Communist forces; nor did they entail
U.S. intervention or a U.S.-Soviet confrontation, with the
possible exception of competing military assistance and veiled
threats of intervention in the 1973 Arab-Israeli war. Yet all
of these major interstate wars gained political significance from
their relationship to the overarching cold war conflict.

Clearly, therefore, the cold war was—and continues to be—
a period of continual limited warfare, and much of this warfare was directly or indirectly a part of the cold war. For this
reason alone limited war deserved the attention it received.
But this does not, in itself, explain the resurgence of limited-
war theories and doctrines and their central role in U.S. foreign
policy. It does not explain why these theories and doctrines
were preoccupied with the *limitation* of war. After all, almost
all local wars of the two kinds were limited for reasons that
need no special explanations. As in previous periods of international conflict, they were limited by the nature of the political
stakes involved and/or the limited military capacity of the
belligerents.

Why, then, did limited war become such a lively conceptual
and operational concern in the cold war? First, the United

States and in lesser degrees major U.S. democratic allies (except where they were directly involved) feared that local wars might become instruments of Communist expansion that could not be contained: indigenous local resistance would be inadequate, and U.S. intervention would either be ineffective in shoring up weak governments or entail too big a risk of Soviet or Chinese counterintervention and nuclear war. Second, there was also fear that U.S. nuclear forces might prove an ineffective deterrent: the growth of the Soviet capacity to devastate the United States and its allies would erode the credibility of U.S. nuclear intervention or retaliaion. In any case, U.S. nuclear weapons might be incapable of preventing local wars that the major Communist powers did not directly initiate or wage with their own forces.

The lesson derived from these twin fears, which dominated strategic thought before the last years of the Vietnam war, was that the military containment of Communist expansion, in order to preserve international order against the prospect of a chain of local aggressions that could lead to World War III, depended on the United States' capacity to help actual and prospective victims withstand Communist aggression and to intervene in their behalf by effective nonnuclear means that would minimize the risk of Soviet or Chinese counterintervention. The subsidiary lesson drawn by some strategists was that, in order to strengthen deterrence or avoid a catastrophic war if deterrence should fail, it was also necessary to enhance the capacity of the United States to use tactical and even strategic nuclear weapons within tolerable limits of physical and human destruction for limited ends.

All the Western postwar theories of limited war are based on these lessons, and are derived from the interaction of the cold war and local conflicts with the fears of nuclear war and the impact of a changing military technology. Looming behind all of them and driving their logic—within the limits of defense budgets, organizational flexibility, and the bounds of plausibility—has been the steadily growing Soviet nuclear capacity to devastate Western Europe and the United States.

As early as 1949, U.S. defense analysts and statesmen began to develop the outlines of the limited-war strategy finally adopted by the Kennedy administration.[3] But the Korean war served as the great catalyst of limited-war thinking and touched off the creative surge of strategic concepts that, along with their accompanying dilemmas and ambiguities, remain a part of our intellectual baggage.

The great impact of the Korean war on Western strategic imagination springs from the fact that the war undermined the preoccupation of strategic thought and plans with general war and challenged the basic premises underlying that preoccupation. The Korean war was a major but local war that occurred at a politically and strategically peripheral point at a time when strategic concepts and plans were dominated by the vision of another general war starting in Europe and by confidence that nuclear deterrence would prevent such a war. Contrary to the whole U.S. conception of fighting a war to completely defeat the enemy with maximum force, the United States found itself seeking only a partial victory while deliberately restricting the nature and scope of its intervention in order to avoid a direct armed encounter with the Soviet Union or a protracted war on the mainland of Asia.

The Korean war, therefore, compelled the proponents of containment to cope with a form of warfare—local conventional war by Soviet proxy—that could be neither deterred nor won by U.S. central-war capacity. At the time, the Western allies were just beginning to anticipate the long-run erosion of U.S. nuclear deterrence by the growth of the Soviet Union's capacity to reach the United States with nuclear weapons. The Korean war raised the specter of a series of local Communist proxy aggressions all around the periphery of the Sino-Soviet bloc, and for a time it raised active fears in the United States and among its European allies that Western Europe might also become the victim of conventional aggression unless the allies greatly strengthened their capacity for local conventional resistance. Although the fear of local proxy wars rapidly diminished and economic stringencies drove the NATO powers to stress nuclear deterrence as an alternative to building up conventional forces for local resistance, the rationale of a Western limited-war strategy persisted. Indeed, limited-war strategy thrived on opposition to the prevailing Eisenhower-Dulles strategy of increased reliance on nuclear deterrence bolstered by military alliances and entered a great period of intellectual creativity, cultivated in the United States and England by a host of academic analysts, army and navy strategists, civilian planners, and research organizations.[4] When President Kennedy came into office, he made the buildup of limited-war capabilities a major step toward fulfilling his campaign pledge to restore U.S. power and prestige around the world and meet the new necessities of containment in a new phase of the cold war, in which the Third World was regarded as the decisive arena of competition between the free world and international communism.

The Theory and Rationale

At the height of limited-war thinking and planning in the United States during the Kennedy period, the theory of limited war was applied to three kinds of wars: local or theater war between states; unconventional or internal war; and strategic or central war, involving the homelands of the United States and the Soviet Union. In each kind of limited war the theory addressed three functions of military strategy: deterrence (the prevention of a military attack and war); denial (the defeat of a military attack); and political support (the support of national policy in situations short of war, ranging from crises to allied relations and the diplomacy of containment). With respect to each kind of limited war a rough consensus developed, though not without significant unresolved differences of opinion and emphasis within the United States and between the United States and its European allies. In each case strategic consensus was accompanied by a good deal of uncertainty, ambiguity, and controversy.

The strategic uncertainties, ambiguities, and controversies were fundamentally the result of the multiple and often conflicting purposes that limited-war strategy was supposed to serve: credible deterrence based on the threat of local war expanding to general nuclear war, but also maximum limitation of war and assured control of escalation; effective denial through conventional defense, but economy of defense expenditures and manpower; geographical restriction of local war, but the minimization of damage to the countries defended in a local war; retention of the confidence and cooperation of allies by convincing them that local defense will be coupled to the U.S. strategic nuclear deterrent, but reduction of the risk that a local war to defend allies will become a central war involving the superpowers; exploitation of new technology to save manpower and facilitate limitation, but avoidance of weapons innovations that might jeopardize arms control agreements and stimulate the arms race. Strategic theories aspire to serve all of these purposes but obviously must choose and compromise among them.

In choosing and compromising among objectives that are equally valid in logic, moreover, strategists operate in a field of human interaction that is full of hypotheses untested and largely untestable by experience. Thus no one knows what would actually happen if tactical nuclear weapons were used in various ways under various conditions. No one can prove the validity of a strategy of deterrence if the event to be deterred does not occur; no one can prove that an alternative would be better if it is not tried; and if the event occurs, no one can be sure that a particular deterrent failed (since the event might have occurred anyway) or that an alternative would have succeeded. Furthermore, as a test of war-fighting theories, an actual armed conflict is likely to be as inconclusive or misleading as the absence of war, since every war is the result of a multiplicity of factors combined in ways that are unique to that conflict and since the strategy that may or may not have worked under one set of circumstances might produce a different outcome under other circumstances. Consequently, the rough consensus on limited-war strategy that has emerged over the years represents logical speculation and inference, shaped more by politics and psychology than by science and evidence; and therefore the claims of competing strategic objectives and theories are free to reassert themselves in new forms that are always plausible in logic and unverifiable in practice.

One division among limited-war strategists, operating in this clouded realm of logical speculation, is between those who emphasize the value of effective denial within controlled limitations and those who emphasize deterring the adversary or bringing him to terms by punitive threats and blows that impose unacceptable costs. Controversies about strategy have often turned on this difference of emphasis. The first emphasis has generally prevailed but has never resolved the doubts and ambiguities inherent in its triumph. As a guide to military policies, denial strategies have the problem of coping with growing Soviet war-fighting capabilities. Both denial and punitive strategies run up against the apparent unresponsiveness of Soviet doctrine to the logic of controlled limitation.

Among the proponents of denial strategies there is another division between those who emphasize limiting war and those who emphasize winning it. Academic theorists are foremost in the first group, professional military men in the second. The "limiters," fearing the natural tendency of military objectives to follow their own logic, have stressed the elaboration of measures of control and mutual restraint designed to keep war from becoming catastrophic. The "winners," relying principally on geographical and political limitations, have stressed the need to be able to defeat enemy forces at every level of war.

In one crucial respect, however, the theory of limited war was largely taken for granted by all strategists of limited war before Vietnam: its political rationale as an instrument of containment. It is remarkable that limited war as an instrument of containment should have become so generally accepted under the Kennedy administration's aegis, whereas it had aroused such strong opposition during the Korean war and in the

Eisenhower-Dulles administration that followed. Perhaps acceptance came so readily because, as an abstract theory designed to deter and cope with future contingencies, the strategy of limited war seemed to cost little while promising simultaneously to strengthen containment and reduce the danger of nuclear war.

The war in Vietnam revived some of the original doubts and controversies about the utility of limited war. It called into question in the 1970s some of the basic assumptions about U.S. interests and power and about domestic political support that underlay the ascendance of limited-war strategy in the 1960s. Yet in many significant ways the strategy transcended the Vietnam war and not only survived it but continued to expand in application and acceptance because its basic rationale was broader than containment.

Although the principal stimulus of limited-war strategy was the perceived imperative of military containment in the nuclear age, the underlying rationale, as expounded by academic analysts and public leaders, transcended the cold war. It rested on the Clausewitzian principle that armed force must serve national policy and therefore, lest it follow its own rules to the physical limits of violence, must be restrained and controlled in order to serve specific political objectives of the state by the use of means proportionate and appropriate to the political stakes and circumstances. The purpose of war, according to this principle, could not be simply to apply maximum force toward the military defeat of the adversary; rather, it must be to employ force skillfully along a continuous spectrum—from diplomacy, to crises short of war, to an overt clash of arms—in order to exert the desired effect upon the adversary's will.

This principle held an appealing logic for the new breed of U.S. liberal realists who had discovered the duty of managing power shrewdly in behalf of world order. It promised to make U.S. power more effective, yet safer. And for those who were not attracted by the enhancement of military security, the fear that a local crisis or war might expand into a nuclear holocaust also provided a compelling motive for limiting warfare. In either case, the rationale called for developing alternatives to the strategy of general war, which had dominated U.S. experience in the twentieth century. In the context of the 1960s this meant developing armed forces capable of flexible and controlled responses to a variety of possible political and military contingencies. The U.S. president must also be provided with a reliable communications, command, and control system that would enable him to tailor force to serve specific political purposes under varied conditions of combat.

This basic rationale, driven by an inner logic and the continued growth of Soviet nuclear striking power, was extended to the calculated, measured use of force throughout the whole spectrum of conflict from armed crises to central nuclear war. The conduct of limited war came to be seen as part of a general "strategy of conflict" in which adversaries would bargain with each other through the medium of graduated military responses, within the boundaries of contrived mutual restraints, in order to achieve a negotiated settlement short of mutual destruction.[5] The "escalation" of war—that is, the graduated increase of its scope and intensity—although originally feared as an uncontrollable danger, came to be regarded as a controllable and reversible process by which adversaries would test each other's will and nerve in order to resolve their conflict at a cost reasonably related to the issues at stake.[6] At its outer theoretical reach, this logic was applied to nuclear exchanges in central war.

The Disparity between Concept and Capabilities

The rationale of limited-war strategy and the strategic theories derived from it have, in essence, become ever more widely accepted over the years, notwithstanding the doubts and reservations arising from Vietnam. Ever since the Korean war, however, there has been a gap between strategic doctrine and the operational plans and capabilities for carrying it out. The Kennedy administration made a determined effort to close this gap but only partially succeeded—succeeded enough, perhaps, to encourage intervention on an expanding scale in Vietnam but not enough to make the mode of intervention appropriate to the circumstances.

The basic reason for the disparity between theory and practice is easy to understand and hard to overcome. Strategic theory in the United States is relatively free to respond to perceptions of national interests, the military balance, and domestic and foreign political imperatives, as viewed and promoted by a variety of public and private elites. Operational plans, force acquisitions, and available military capabilities, however, are constrained by the limits of the defense budget, the rising cost of conventional manpower, the technical preferences of the weapons acquisition community and the military managers, and the standard procedures of military organization, training, and the assignment of service missions. Plans, acquisitions, and capabilities are skewed by the virtually autonomous process of technological innovations, which is generated by the military's search for high-performance, multipurpose weapons that promise to substitute firepower for manpower and by the weapons industry's competition for contracts, which plays to this preference. The actual conduct of war is conditioned by the ingrained doctrine, training, and organization of the U.S. military establistment, particularly the U.S. Army, to fight wars by overpowering the adversary's manpower and logistics with massive striking force and attrition—a disposition born of superior resources and technology—although wars of maneuver and mobility may be more effective both militarily and politically.

The danger of the theory/practice disparity is that it encourages the commitment of U.S. power to support national interests in contingencies for which the forms of available power are inadequate or inappropriate. The U.S. military establishment, charged with supporting worldwide commitments, can seldom expect to have enough ready military power to fight the kind of war it prefers, and is therefore extremely conservative both in advising intervention and insisting on maximum manpower and firepower when it cannot avoid intervention. The resulting gap between strategy, on the one hand, and operational plans and capabilities, on the other, may weaken deterrence, undermine the will to fulfill commitments, or (most conspicuously in the case of Vietnam) lead to military failure.

Logically, if capabilities cannot be made adequate and appropriate, the disparity between strategic theory and practice can be overcome in the following ways: (1) by altering military strategy to make its requirements commensurate with capabilities (for example, by increasing reliance on nuclear deterrence instead of conventional or unconventional resistance); (2) by contracting the scope and demands of military containment (as through a more selective definition of vital interests or a greater tolerance of an adversary's efforts to expand his sphere of influence at the expense of these interests); (3) by relying more heavily on other countries to support containment; (4) by relying on diplomacy, supplemented by the levers of economic aid, arms transfers, or arms control, to diminish the threats to containment. To one degree or another, at various times, the United States has resorted to each of these methods; but all of these methods together have not completely closed the gap between strategy and capabilities in the past, and there is no assurance that they will do so in the future.

The growing strength and reach of Soviet conventional power, combined with the deepening inhibitions in the West against relying on nuclear responses to supplant conventional ones, tend to preclude the adjustment of strategy to suit capabilities. The reaction of the military establishment to the frustrations of Vietnam, the mounting costs of military manpower, and the diminished public support for armed intervention obstruct the adjustment of capabilities to suit strategy. The proliferation of local conflicts and of other threats to regional stability and international order bodes ill for narrowing the disparity between the theory and practice of limited-war strategy by diplomatic means. What devolution of military power and initiative has taken place seems as likely to complicate as to facilitate containment. The post-Vietnam relaxation of containment is challenged by rising turbulence in the Third World and the evident determination of the Soviet Union to exploit it. A lasting relaxation of containment evidently depends more on hopeful but fallible assumptions about the limits of Moscow's intention and ability to exploit opportunities for aggrandizement than on U.S. tolerance of Soviet success. As events in Asia and Africa challenge these assumptions, U.S. tolerance tends to give way to cold-war fears.

Three Types
of Limited-War Strategy

Local War

Limited-war strategy in the early 1960s applied preeminently to local conventional war, since this was the kind of limited war that the United States had experienced in Korea, that was congruent with the U.S. emphasis, in military doctrine and organization, on firepower and attrition, and that was integrally related to the West's most important security interests in Western Europe.

The strategy of local conventional war started with the premise that the growth of the Soviet capacity to devastate the United States with nuclear weapons would lead to a situation of strategic parity in which the Soviet Union as well as the United States could inflict unacceptable damage upon each other no matter which struck first. In this situation, which was perceived to be as much a matter of psychology as capabilities, the credibility of the United States' willingness to use nuclear weapons to protect even its most important allies, if they could not be protected conventionally, would inevitably erode.

Not only would this situation undermine deterrence and make local conventional aggression more likely, but it would also weaken NATO, the most important international sinew of containment. Strategic parity would raise doubts as to whether the United States would defend its allies by retaliating with nuclear strikes against Soviet forces at the risk of incurring the penalty of a Soviet nuclear assault against the United States. U.S. allies would fear that allied land would become a nuclear battleground if the United States did use nuclear weapons. If the president, therefore, had no choice but humiliation or holocaust, he might lack the nerve for tough bargaining in crises or he might run improvident risks of war. Finally, if the United States or its allies and other friendly countries became involved in a local war because deterrence was ineffective or inapplicable, as would be most likely in the so-called "grey areas" not clearly protected by U.S. military alliances, the West, unable to deny the aggressor a victory by conventional means, could only face defeat or resort to a desperate nuclear response.

It followed, according to the strategic logic of the Kennedy administration, that the United States, in order to avoid these military and political dangers, must have forces that could raise the "nuclear threshold" in Europe by helping raise NATO's level of conventional resistance and provide a range of conventional military options to cope with a variety of contingencies—from the "management" of crises, to the containment of "brushfire" wars, to the waging of a large-scale war in Europe. Achieving these options would put a premium on mobility, readiness, and effective command and control. Conventional forces, according to projections of a "two-and-a-half war" capability (that was never achieved), would have to be powerful enough not only to fight a large-scale protracted war in Europe, but also—because of assumptions about a Sino-Soviet bloc that were already outmoded in the 1960s—to cope with a major local war in Asia and have something left over for a crisis or brushfire war in the Caribbean or some peripheral area.

The strategy of conventional local war raised several questions to which there could be no definitive answers, with or without an empirical test. One question concerned the relation of deterrence to denial. If the conventional denial capabilities of NATO were strengthened, would this weaken their deterrent effect by indicating to the adversary that the United States was afraid to use nuclear weapons? Or would this strengthen deterrence by convincing the adversary that he would have to fight a large-scale war, which would entail a larger risk of nuclear war than a small encounter or a quick military *fait accompli*? The European allies, aware of their relative geographical vulnerability, hard-pressed politically to maintain conventional force levels (particularly because of rising manpower costs), and anxious to do nothing to diminish the credibility of their U.S. nuclear umbrella, posed the first question. Yet they more or less acceded to U.S. pressure for defense contributions as long as Washington buttressed its affirmative answer to the second question by repeated assurances that U.S. troops would stay on NATO's central front to guarantee that the United States would regard an attack on its allies as an attack on itself.

On paper and in doctrine the U.S. strategy—flexible response and enhanced conventional capabilities to raise the nuclear threshold—prevailed and was finally embodied, although with numerous concessions to allied anxieties, in NATO's official strategic posture statement (MC 14/3) in December 1967.[1] In reality, however, this did not resolve the question about the effect of denial capabilities on deterrence, which continued to underlie the issue of how much and what kind of conventional capabilities NATO needed or could be expected to get. Since this controversy could never be settled with logic, both sides in the issue showed some ambivalence, and the resulting compromise reflected domestic and international politics more than theoretical speculation.

Closely related to the question about the relation of deterrence to denial were doubts about the feasibility of offsetting, with conventional forces, the Warsaw Pact's advantages of geography, military initiative, and mobilized manpower. For if the presumed East-West imbalance of forces really could not be significantly redressed, the NATO allies would be no more secure after going to the great trouble and cost of a fruitless competition in conventional forces. U.S. defense officials in the 1960s tried to convince allied governments that estimates of the East's inherent combat superiority publicized in the

1950s were inflated and that raising the relative level of NATO's conventional capabilities was feasible. At the same time, defense planners worried about ways that NATO—with its huge military overhead and logistical problems, illogical deployment of national forces, duplication of weapons systems, and vulnerable communications network and airfields—might get more fighting power for its money.

The feasibility of a large-scale local war was not only a question of military effectiveness, however, it was also a question of whether such a war could really be limited. The Korean war demonstrated, contrary to prevailing Western strategic concepts and plans, that even a major clash of regular military units— World War II writ small—could be limited geographically, militarily, and politically, despite the direct participation of the United States and China and the indirect participation of the Soviet Union. But although the sudden fear in the West that the North Korean invasion might be the model for aggression in Central Europe quickly subsided, there remained considerable doubt—especially in Western Europe, where the difference between a Korean-type limited war and another general war seemed less significant than in the United States—that a war on the Korean scale in an area of such decisive interest to the superpowers could remain significantly limited, even if both sides wished to avoid another world war. This doubt reinforced the question, with very practical implications for defense expenditures and manpower policies: If a large-scale limited war in Europe is unlikely, why go to the cost and political trouble of preparing for it and incur the risk of weakening the deterrent effect of the prospect that such a war would rapidly escalate to central war?

In practice, the answer was a compromise. Although some strategists, particularly in the United States during Secretary of Defense Robert W. McNamara's regime, preferred to rely on NATO's ability to fight a large-scale local conventional war rather than depend on any strategy of limited options beyond the nuclear threshold,[2] this strategy failed to gain much foreign or domestic support. The prevailing strategic concept in the United States and Western Europe, conveyed with all the ambiguities of a collective agreement in MC 14/3, envisioned a Korean-type war in Europe escalating to a general war within a few weeks. Whether NATO's plans and capabilities were any more appropriate for a general nuclear war than for a large-scale conventional war was another question, but this question was easier to ignore when the United States retained a significant superiority in intercontinental striking power (before the 1970s). Backed by U.S. nuclear superiority, the prospect of escalation, not the avoidance of it, remained the crux of NATO's deterrent strategy. At most, NATO's conventional forces, if confronted by a major attack, might enforce a "pause" for negotiating a termination of hostilities before war ascended the "escalation ladder." How this pause differed from a "tripwire" on U.S. nuclear retaliation, which had been a popular concept in the 1950s, depended on how long NATO forces might be expected to withstand a determined Warsaw Pact attack; and, on this question, estimates ranged widely from a few days to several months.

To keep local wars of various magnitudes limited in areas outside the protection of NATO or the security treaty with Japan would depend, according to the prevailing view, on limiting the political objectives of the war (principally, to preserving the independence and territory of the country attacked) and carefully relating these objectives to limits on the war's geographical extent and its weapons and their targets. Above all, these limitations should be designed to avoid direct Soviet or Chinese intervention, even at the price of granting local aggressors military sanctuaries. Apart from geographical restriction, the clearest and most compelling standard of limitation was believed to be the nonuse of nuclear weapons. In Europe, just where this dividing line (or "firebreak," as its advocates called it) should be drawn was the source of strategic doubts and controversies that persist to this day. Outside Europe the credibility (in U.S. eyes) of initiating the use of nuclear weapons under any circumstances seemed to reach a high point in 1954 during the Quemoy and Matsu crisis and the fall of Dienbienphu and has steadily declined ever since.

Entangled with both the question of the relation between deterrence and denial and the question of feasible limitation was the chronic question about the role of tactical, or battle-field, nuclear weapons (TNW). In the 1960s this question, too, had reference primarily to the European theater, although the option of using tactical nuclear weapons against staging bases and other military targets in Korea and elsewhere—an option which was part of Secretary of State Dulles's supposedly rejected strategy of avoiding future Korean wars—remained alive.

Tactical nuclear weapons were originally included in NATO strategy in 1953 in order to compensate, by substituting firepower for manpower, for the shortfall in meeting the post-Korean war force goals that were projected as necessary for an effective forward defense.[3] Any war in Europe was expected to be nuclear, so TNW were to be used from the outset. President Eisenhower, Secretary of State Dulles, and others said that nuclear weapons had achieved conventional status. As late as 1960 operational plans for using the several thousand TNW that had been deployed in Europe still treated TNW almost as conventional weapons. However, with the rising consciousness of the destructive effects of nuclear weapons and of growing Soviet nuclear strength since the late 1950s, TNW have generally come to be regarded more as weapons of deterrence than as adjuncts to conventional denial—slightly less dangerous and therefore more credible than strategic nuclear weapons. They seem to provide a necessary step between a conventional local war and nuclear central war, but there has never been agreement on a plausible doctrine for keeping a local nuclear war limited. TNW are regarded as a necessary step up the nuclear escalation ladder, but they, too, are affected by growing inhibitions regarding the first use of nuclear weapons against a conventional attack, which have steadily diminished the credibility of strategic nuclear retaliation.

The effort of strategists to harness TNW to local war reached a logical extreme in the theories of limited tactical nuclear war propounded by Admiral Sir Anthony Buzzard in 1956 and by Henry Kissinger in 1957.[4] But in both instances confidence in tactical nuclear warfare as a more effective form of local resistance soon waned, and these theories were never widely accepted or officially implemented.

Most official studies and war games indicated that, even if it could be limited geographically, a tactical nuclear war in Europe would probably produce such chaos as to be beyond predictable control, that it would devastate the European allies, and that it would require more rather than less manpower. Moreover, given the growing Soviet TNW force, NATO's ports, airfields, supplies, and logistics seemed particularly vulnerable in a tactical nuclear war. Nor could the presumed advantage of TNW for defense be counted on to help NATO, since the defending countries would be faced with the task of going on the offense in order to remove the attacking forces from allied territory.

The elaboration of nuclear local-war strategies, therefore, was left largely to the ingenious but esoteric theories of bargaining, controlled escalation, reprisals, "shots across the bow," and demonstrations propounded by Herman Kahn and Thomas Schelling. But, considering West European nuclear fears, the constraints on democratic governments, and the problems of coordinating nuclear decisions among allies, there was no reason to think that the NATO powers would have the advantage in nuclear bargaining, particularly since the Soviet Union would probably follow a nuclear demonstration with nuclear retaliation aimed at exerting a military effect.[5] Since there was an equal lack of confidence in NATO's ability to either limit or win a large-scale conventional war in such a vital area as Western Europe, the function of TNW became primarily one of deterrence through threat of escalation. As such, TNW became the source of a certain tension of strategic emphases between the United States, which alone could authorize the use of nuclear weapons, and U.S. allies. The United States became more interested in reducing the risk that the use of TNW would lead to a central nuclear war; the allies became more concerned that "decoupling" TNW from U.S. strategic forces would reduce their credibility as a deterrent.

Some concluded that NATO's dilemma—relying on a great quantity of battlefield weapons that were an indispensable supplement to conventional resistance but an unreliable instrument of local war and that were a necessary step short of strategic nuclear retaliation but increasingly incredible as a prelude to central war—could only be mitigated by technological innovations making tactical nuclear weapons less destructive and more discriminating through lower explosive yield, reduced radiation, or reduced blast. But these innovations encountered the objection that they would tend to cloud or eliminate the firebreak between nuclear and conventional weapons, which, it was argued, is the clearest and the most indispensable criterion for preserving mutual limitations on war, especially when the belligerents are nuclear powers.

One trouble with all strategies of local war in Europe is that the Soviet Union has shown virtually no inclination to be a partner to them. Rather, Soviet doctrine, published commentaries, and war maneuvers have seemed rigidly geared to a strategy of blitzkrieg—a sudden offensive strike with conventional and nuclear (both battlefield and strategic) weapons intended to defeat and disorganize the NATO powers. Although Soviet military writings in the late 1960s envisaged the possibility of limited nonnuclear exchanges, they remained invariably hostile to ideas of controlled escalation and intrawar bargaining by limited options of any kind, and especially by nuclear options.

One can argue that Soviet declaratory strategy is a form of psychological warfare and that Soviet leaders, being politically rational and cautious in the use of force, would follow the U.S. logic of limitation when actually faced with war rather than incur the extravagant costs of a general nuclear war. But the weight of evidence indicates that Soviet strategy, although equally conscious of the danger of unrestricted war and equally open to a variety of less-than-total responses, follows a different logic. Dominated by military officers, who are conditioned by historical memories that place a premium on quantitative superiority and the sudden massive offensive, Soviet strategic thinking is overwhelmingly directed toward the "winners' " objective of defeating enemy forces quickly with all necessary means. Convinced that preparing for war and waging it must be based on a military science that follows the objective laws of armed conflict, Soviet strategists see a direct logical progression from strategy, to doctrine, to weapons and forces, to operations, a progression that contrasts significantly with the U.S. penchant for diversified capabilities and tactical improvisation to meet unpredictable circumstances and that leads to a method of "scientific military management" unreceptive to the kind of political and psychological intuitions that intrigue U.S. limited-war strategists.[6] But the difference between the Soviet and U.S. strategic logic is not primarily that the former stresses war-fighting and the latter deterrence—both stress deterrence as the proper objective of nuclear strategy—nor even that the former bases deterrence more on operational war-fighting capabilities. The principal difference is that U.S. nuclear strategy rests on an explicit theory of conflict-control and bargaining, whereas Soviet nuclear strategic doctrine rests on operational concepts of employing nuclear weapons to exert military effects and is thoroughly skeptical of the feasibility of controlling nuclear exchanges as bargaining levers. To U.S. civilian strategists the cardinal principle of Clausewitz—that armed force must serve political ends—requires the scrupulous limitation of nuclear options. To Soviet military strategists the same principle requires eschewing illusions about the limitability of nuclear warfare, which they believe beg the question of what drastic political purposes and circumstances would justify the recourse to nuclear war in the first place.[7]

Given this contrast in Soviet and U.S. strategic outlooks, deeply rooted in cultural, political, and historical differences, all the Western strategies of local war in Europe have suffered from the implication that they serve primarily to ameliorate the NATO countries' own psychological and political problems rather than to induce the adversary to observe the rules of limitation. Since one can argue that allied cohesion, on the basis of whatever strategic compromise, enhances deterrence, there is something to be said for formulating strategy to suit the allies even if the Warsaw Pact may not play the game. But if Soviet relative military capabilities continue to increase at every level of warfare—nuclear as well as conventional and theater as well as central war—the danger will arise that allied acceptance of the U.S. logic of limitation will simply undermine the credibility of an inexorably escalating nuclear first-use strategy while NATO's capacity to win *any* kind of war declines.

Unconventional War

The strategy of local resistance—despite or because of its ambiguities, the unanswered and probably unanswerable questions it raised, and the disparities between strategic concept and operational plans and capabilities—did, in its essentials, become an enduring aspect of the general policy of containment, transcending the particular phase of the cold war during which it emerged. Local resistance as a strategy even survived the Vietnam war, although the international political environment and some of the key assumptions about it changed and, because of those changes, bred confusion and uncertainty about the contingencies under which the United States or its allies might engage in such a war.

By contrast, the intense U.S. preoccupation in the 1960s with unconventional or internal war and a strategy of counterinsurgency quickly dissolved in the agonies of the war in Vietnam, overshadowed by a large-scale conventional war of attrition. As in the case of strategies of local interstate war, the strategy of counterinsurgency attained prominence as a reflection of the interests of the United States—and, before that, of France—in a particular period of history. It declined into obscurity when the United States, in reaction to the Vietnam trauma, lost confidence in the utility of any armed intervention as an instrument of containment in the Third World.

There have been a great many internal wars since World War II—that is, wars fought within a state (though usually assisted from outside) for the control of a people and government through guerrilla warfare, terrorism, insurrection, or subversion—but until recently relatively few interstate wars between regular military units. Nevertheless, internal wars did not concern U.S. strategists until the 1960s. Their concern, however, was foreshadowed by French strategists and, in a more tactical sense, by British strategists, who were generalizing their countries' experiences in fighting insurrections in Burma, Malaya, and Indonesia (in the case of Great Britain) and in Indochina and Algeria (in the case of France).

In France the theorists of *la guerre revolutionnaire*, who were mostly professional military officers, expounded a strategy (based on the theory of Mao Tse-tung) of revolutionary war, which they saw as an instrument of Communist expansion serving Soviet interests and designs.[8] Indirect aggression by revolutionary war, they contended, was an insidious substitute for *la guerre classique*. If it were not contained, it would lead to Soviet hegemony or World War III, just as the chain of Fascist aggression led to World War II.

Despite a similarity of conceptual frameworks, these French strategists had practically no influence on U.S. advocates of limited-war strategy, who were predominantly political scientists reacting to the lessons of the Korean war. In the United States the lesson drawn from the French experience, by Senator John F. Kennedy among others, was a political one: counterinsurgency had failed because it was not sufficiently responsive to the need to build an indigenous nationalist anti-Communist base of operations. Nor did the U.S. experience of assisting counterinsurgencies in Greece, the Philippines, Guatemala, or Cuba affect U.S. strategic theory until the 1960s, when counterinsurgency came to be seen as a major means of combating a grave threat to U.S. security. The U.S. strategy of counterinsurgency arose in the mid-1950s from the perception of U.S.

statesmen and strategists that the Sino-Soviet bloc, having been contained on the level of regular local interstate war, was actively exploiting less risky, more effective means of Communist expansion through "indirect aggression" based on the support of local guerrilla action and subversion. But whereas Secretary of State Dulles had merely identified this form of aggression as part of a new and dangerous phase of the cold war, President Kennedy came into office determined to do something about it.

From the beginning the president and his brother Robert personally took the lead in developing and implementing a strategy of counterinsurgency in order to prevent and defeat "wars of national liberation," as the Communists called them. Chairman Khrushchev's declaration just before Kennedy's inauguration that these wars, unlike a general nuclear war, were inevitable and that Communists must support them as "just wars" may have been primarily a response to increasingly strident Chinese criticisms of Soviet unwillingness to provide moral and tangible support to the needs of foreign Communist parties. But coming in the wake of revolutionary wars in South Vietnam, Cuba, and Algeria, not to mention lingering memories of the "loss of China," and coinciding with a presidential campaign that promised to arouse the United States from the lethargies of the Eisenhower regime and mobilize its power to meet the Communist challenge in the Third World, Khrushchev's pronouncement became the catalyst for a new direction in strategic doctrine and plans.

This doctrine, as publicly espoused by Walt Rostow, Roger Hilsman, and U. Alexis Johnson and officially promulgated in National Security Action Memorandums (NSAMs) 124 and 182 of August 1962,[9] postulated a coordinated Sino-Soviet strategy for advancing Communist power in the Third World. Avoiding the risk of a direct military confrontation, the Sino-Soviet bloc, according to this analysis, had conspired to exploit the political and economic dissatisfactions and the indigenous nationalist ambitions of peoples who, seized by the "revolution of rising expectations," were determined to modernize their countries and free them from foreign domination. To defeat this threat to U.S. security, democratic principles, and international order the United States would have to adopt a strategy of integrating economic and political development along democratic lines with counterinsurgency efforts in order to enable threatened governments to eliminate the roots of popular discontent and suppress guerrilla attacks upon their freedom.

This might require the United States to strengthen beleaguered governments—even to reform them—by giving them economic, administrative, and internal security assistance; but there was no expectation that Americans themselves would be involved in counterinsurgent wars except as advisors, trainers, and, if necessary, adjuncts to local forces. For U.S. forces to assume direct responsibility for combat would be to fall into the fatal French misconception that external forces could win insurgencies. Yet President Kennedy insisted upon a wide array of counterinsurgency programs throughout the armed services, which required a radical revision of weapons, tactics, and organization in order to meet the new challenge. Although the regular armed services, with the possible exception of the marines, never in fact came close to this kind of revision, the confidence and enthusiasm of the time, inspired by the president's leadership, infected civilian security leaders and some military officers who shared their outlook with a determination to demonstrate that the United States could also cope with this form of aggression within the constraints of limited war.

Central War

The most intractable dilemma of military strategy in the nuclear age—with a particularly grim moral as well as material dimension—is that the principal nuclear antagonists must ultimately base their security on a nuclear threat which, if carried out, would probably inflict a magnitude of destruction on themselves as well as on others that could scarcely be justified by any rational reason for resorting to war. Should the resulting unprecedented inhibition against war fail, there looms a threat to civilization itself.

The dilemma may be psychologically tolerable in proportion to the improbability of a strategic nuclear war. But for some analysts of deterrence even the slightest chance of such a mutually catastrophic war should compel statesmen to limit the extent of destruction. Moreover, the fact that a major function of U.S. nuclear deterrent forces is to deter conventional or tactical nuclear attacks upon allies accentuates the dilemma by placing the responsibility for starting a strategic nuclear war on the United States.

Americans concerned about military security must square the burden of nuclear deterrence with the public conscience (or at least with their own consciences). Hence it is understandable that, given the rising inhibition against nuclear war and the persistent desire for military containment, some strategists should look to the logic of limited war to mitigate the dilemma of strategic nuclear deterrence—although this logic has been condemned by Soviet spokesmen and has received no encouragement from U.S. allies. Their objective has been to devise a strategy of U.S.-Soviet nuclear exchange, supported by the proper kinds and quantities of weapons, operational plans, and an effective communications, command, and control system (C^3), that would enable the United States to use its strategic nuclear capacity with sufficient moderation and discrimination to end a war for a limited political aim while avoiding unacceptable damage.

Strategies of limited central war have had two major functions. One is to enhance the credibility of nuclear retaliation against the Soviet Union in response to conventional aggressions against countries the United States wants to protect—a function sometimes called "extended deterrence." The other is to limit damage by making any nuclear war in which the United States and its allies might become involved—whether in response to conventional aggression, a deliberate Soviet first strike, or because of accident or miscalculation—subject to political control and a political termination short of catastrophic destruction. Related to these two functions is a third: limited central war as a strategy provides the U.S. president with a military basis for conducting diplomacy during crises (as in Berlin) that allows greater resolve, greater flexibility, and also greater allied confidence in U.S. firmness and prudence than a strategy in which nuclear encounter is necessarily tantamount to unlimited mutual destruction.

The first function—deterrence—as in the strategy of local conventional war, was applied to strategies of central war as a way of escaping the seeming contradiction between Secretary of State Dulles's declared strategy of relying more heavily on U.S. capacity to inflict so-called "massive retaliation" to deter local conventional wars and a growing consciousness that the increasing destructive power and invulnerability of U.S. and Soviet nuclear strategic forces were undermining the feasibility of either side striking the other first without receiving unacceptable retaliatory damage.[10] Agreeing that the United States could not do without the deterrent effect of a strategic nuclear response to conventional aggression, critics of the Dulles strategy nevertheless claimed that this kind of deterrence was becoming ineffective against anything but a large-scale conventional attack in the most vital areas, and perhaps only in Western Europe. And even in Western Europe it was losing its credibility. To make this extended deterrence more credible, or at least not incredible, the critics advocated a strategy to render nuclear exchanges more limited in destructiveness, more discriminating in targets, and more susceptible to political control for the sake of sensible limited ends. Most advocates viewed this strategy not as a substitute for conventional resistance, which they advocated strengthening, but as a means of rationalizing the existing strategy.

In the 1960s there were two principal schools of limited central nuclear war strategy. One, expounded most notably by Herman Kahn in *On Thermonuclear War* (1960) and *Thinking About the Unthinkable* (1962), condemned the current conception of nuclear war as an uncontrolled "spasm" and urged a counterforce strategy with a city-avoidance option, which, combined with civil and air defense, could confine Soviet retaliatory damage to limits that would make the U.S. policy of strategic nuclear response to a major Soviet aggression against Western Europe rational to carry out and more effective as a deterrent. The other school, developed by Leo Szilard, Thomas Schelling, Morton Kaplan, and others, sought the same objective through a strategy of bargaining with limited strategic reprisals on targets of civilian rather than primarily military value.[11]

The second school of limited central war strategy was too esoteric, improbable, and beyond the range of normal military thinking to receive much attention. The first school, largely because of Kahn's provocative way of expounding it, attracted a great deal of public attention. It was intensely criticized on the grounds that such an approach was inhumane because it dealt so callously with the calculus of "megadeaths" and that it was destabilizing because it would make the first use of nuclear weapons (perhaps even preemptively or preventively) more likely and because it would accelerate the arms race by stimulating a competition in counterforce weapons. In the Kennedy administration, however, this strategy was partially accepted in theory as part of the general emphasis on flexible and controlled responses. Secretary of Defense Robert McNamara stated on several occasions the value of having among general-war options a counterforce, reciprocal city-avoidance, damage-limiting strategy more or less along the lines of Kahn's preferred option.[12]

On the other hand, these statements were not backed by a detailed doctrine of employment or by operational plans for the limited use of strategic nuclear weapons.[13] Moreover, the government soon abandoned its declaratory policy, perhaps partly in response to domestic dissent as well as to budgetary restraint, and emphasized instead the stabilization of the strategic nuclear balance. McNamara and other defense spokesmen avoided justifying the limitation of strategic war on the grounds of making a nuclear first strike less costly and more politically useful. In fact, they reinforced the stigma against the initial use of nuclear weapons by arguing that "mutual assured destruction," based on U.S. and Soviet possession of large invulnerable strategic forces making a first strike unacceptably costly because of second-strike retaliation, was the necessary basis for stabilizing and controlling the arms race. A counter-force strategy, Secretary McNamara explained, would not make the resort to nuclear war by either side more attractive. It would only limit damage if a nuclear war occurred. Furthermore, it was unlikely, he conceded, that the Soviet Union would play the game of bargaining with measured counterforce strikes while avoiding cities.

The Kennedy and Johnson administrations continued to apply the concept of flexible and controlled response to central war strategy to the extent of studying multiple strategic nuclear options and improving the strategic command and control system. But they fell far short of formulating or implementing either a plausible first-strike or second-strike strategy of limited nuclear central war that had the support of the military bureaucracy. One logical element of a flexible and controlled response strategy, civil defense, ran into so much public opposition—both in its passive form, fallout shelters, and its active form, antiballistic missiles—that it was abandoned by the government. The debate and furor over these programs showed that, however frightful the hypothetical resort to a suicidal spasm war might be, the public was more comfortable with mutual assured destruction (or MAD, as its critics would later call it) than with efforts to make strategic nuclear war more usable—at least, if those efforts were *visible* reminders that a nuclear war might actually be fought and not just deterred. As for mitigating the nuclear dilemma, the only popular measures were détente and strategic nuclear arms control.

Neither the Soviet government nor U.S. European allies showed any interest in mitigating the nuclear dilemma by strategies of limited central war. After the death of Stalin, Soviet strategists apparently did abandon the view that a general war would be just a more destructive World War II, and some spokesmen conceded that the Soviet Union could not win a general war without the "annihilation of almost all life" in both camps (as Khrushchev put it). But Soviet nuclear plans evidently continued to call for a massive strike at cities and military targets simultaneously, and Soviet spokesmen continued to insist that the USSR must and would prevail in a strategic nuclear war by virtue of its superior war-fighting ability. Soviet leaders denied the possibility of a controlled nuclear war and condemned U.S. strategies of limited strategic war as provocative and destabilizing. Although this position was surely intended to serve a psychological and political purpose by keeping nuclear fears and inhibitions alive in the West, turning these fears against the United States, and depreciating U.S. nuclear protection of its European allies, one must assume, in the face of the evidence, that the Soviet position also reflected the state of Soviet operational plans and strategic forces.[14] Although attainment of strategic parity and an invulnerable retaliatory force might yet lead Soviet strategists to apply to central war their general Clausewitzian approach to force as an instrument of policy, their strategic outlook seemed impervious to this U.S. logic in the 1960s and remains so today.

The European allies also remained impervious to the logic of controlled strategic war. From the U.S. standpoint West Europeans should have welcomed any strategy that made a nuclear first strike in their behalf more credible by strengthening the U.S. president's will to carry it out. In reality, however, Europeans who followed military strategic issues were far more interested in the credibility of tactical nuclear responses to conventional attacks and met U.S. concerns about limiting strategic war with indifference or skepticism. Some suspected that such concerns were another indication that the United States might not be willing to sacrifice its own cities in order to protect Europe, and they wondered if the superpowers might conspire to limit their own damage while Europe bore the brunt of the destruction.

The Lessons of Vietnam

The Rationale of Intervention

If the early 1960s saw the height of enthusiasm for limited war as an instrument of U.S. policy, the late 1960s witnessed, in Vietnam, the greatest blow to that enthusiasm. The impact of the blow was accentuated by the fact that it came in the Third World, where the Kennedy administration saw the greatest danger to U.S. interests and the greatest opportunity to protect them by applying a strategy of limited war.

The failure of limited war in Vietnam was bound to affect the U.S. strategic outlook, just as the success of limited war in Korea had shaped the strategic outlook that contributed so much to U.S. intervention in Vietnam.[1] But the nature and scope of the strategic reaction to the Vietnam war, like the reaction to the Korean war, was to be determined not only by the experience of the war itself but also by the impact of the changing international environment on perceptions of U.S. security interests, the external threats to these interests, and the role of U.S. military power in countering these threats.

Ten years after U.S. disaffection with the war in Vietnam, marked by North Vietnam's Tet offensive in 1968, the war's impact had been profound, yet not nearly as drastic as many observers predicted at the time of U.S. withdrawal. The impact of Vietnam on limited-war strategy was concentrated on the use of limited war as an instrument of containment in the Third World, and here the political conclusions drawn from the

Vietnam experience (though by no means definitive) were much clearer than the military lessons. This is appropriate since the general rationale of the Kennedy strategy of limited war and not the specific military tactics of counterinsurgency had been applied most clearly during the war; and since the political constraints in Vietnam, in the United States, and abroad had most clearly affected the outcome of the military operations.

In retrospect, it seems remarkable how unquestioningly and universally the general political rationale of the war in Vietnam was accepted and the political constraints were ignored. Although the security of Southeast Asian states, unlike the security of Western Europe, was never regarded as intrinsically vital on economic, strategic, or political-cultural grounds, after the Korean war U.S. leaders, with virtually no dissent, defined the security of noncommunist Indochina from Communist aggression as critical to international order and U.S. security. The rationale was that the loss of any country to communism would threaten not only the other countries in the region but also vital U.S. interests in the whole of the Far East and even in the Middle East and Europe. This position was endorsed by President Truman in June 1952, publicly reiterated by President Eisenhower and Secretary of State Dulles before and after France was forced to withdraw from its war against the Vietminh, and declared to be the crucial test of containment by President Kennedy.[2]

Although buttressed by occasional references to the rubber and tin of Southeast Asia, the peninsula's geopolitical position between the Pacific and Indian oceans, and Japan's economic dependence on the region, this portrayal of the Communist threat was still notable for its abstractness. The U.S. stake in Vietnam arose, not from any analysis of concrete interests, but simply from the application of the Truman Doctrine and the general strategy of containment to Asia. This strategy seemed imperative because of China's bellicose advocacy of wars of national liberation and its apparent expansionist intentions, marked by Chinese threats to the offshore islands in 1954 and

1958 and by a border war with India in 1964, and because of the general fear, following the Soviet launching of Sputnik in 1957 and culminating in the Cuban missile crisis of 1962, of an adverse shift toward the Sino-Soviet bloc in the world balance of power.

Given the compelling nature of this general rationale for supporting containment in Vietnam and the resurgent confidence in U.S. power that sprang from President Kennedy's determination to restore the military basis of the U.S. reputation as the guardian of international order, there was little incentive to scrutinize the prospects of the success or failure of limited war. As after the North Korean invasion, there seemed to be no acceptable alternative to armed counterintervention. Despite the bitter French experience, the United States would have to carry on the fight. That was the lesson of the interwar period, from Manchuria to Munich.

Of course, notwithstanding this compelling rationale, no one would have advocated armed intervention if the full cost and the failure that would result had been known. Therefore, Americans must ask where and why this limited war went wrong. Was it the conception or the execution of the war, or both? It will take some time for analysts and polemicists to assess in detail the operational reasons for the cost and failure of the war. But already the popular lessons drawn from Vietnam reflect a profound, if mixed and inconclusive, reappraisal of the rationale of the war. Thus the things taken for granted at the outset are the things most questioned in the aftermath: the nature of U.S. interests, the nature and significance of the Communist threat, and the ability of U.S. military power to defeat Communist incursions in the Third World.

Two predominant views emerge from the lessons drawn from the war and ascribe the unhappy outcome to two different kinds of errors. Some critics, accepting the rationale of U.S. intervention and taking the local political and military conditions as givens, believe that the outcome might have been different and fulfilled the rationale if certain mistakes of

strategy and execution had been avoided. Therefore, they conclude that the United States might have conducted the war differently and won. That is, the United States might have defeated
North Vietnam and achieved the independence of South Vietnam at an acceptable cost. It follows that either the United
States should have fought the war differently or it should not
have intervened at all. Other critics, however, believe that, given
the political and military conditions in Vietnam, the rationale
for intervening was wrong (that is, was contrary to U.S. interests
and principles) and that U.S. goals could not have been achieved
at a reasonable cost by a different strategy. They conclude that
the United States could not have won the war and probably
should not have tried.

Actually, neither view is more plausible than its obverse:
namely, that the rationale of U.S. intervention was misconceived
but the United States might nonetheless have won the war if it
had been bolder, more skillful, or had been willing to make a
greater effort; or that the rationale was valid but there was no
way to win the war, given the weakness of the South Vietnamese
government and society and the limits of U.S. interest and
power in the area. Psychologically, however, the contradiction
and irony of these positions is less appealing. In any case,
whether either verdict is right or both are wrong, no lesson can
tell us much, if anything, that is definitively relevant to future
local wars in which the political and military conditions might
come closer to justifying intervention and be more conducive
to success.

Significantly, neither view categorically rejects intervention,
in some form and under some circumstances, to support containment by means of a limited war. Several key military issues
arose in the Vietnam war from which some lessons that transcend
Vietnam may be derived. These issues pertain to the strategy
and tactics of counterinsurgency, early escalation versus gradualism, controlled and graduated escalation, sanctuaries and other
limits, and the dynamics of large-scale conventional war in
Third World insurgencies. Cutting across these military issues

are the political issues that arose from the effects of political constraints in South Vietnam and the United States on the conduct of the war and pertaining to what, if anything, could have been done about these constraints to promote victory at an acceptable cost. Underlying all these issues is one ultimate question with the broadest relevance to the future of limited-war strategy in the Third World: Did United States interests justify intervention in Vietnam?

The Reasons for Failure

This is not the place nor is it yet the time to try to appraise the errors and successes of Vietnam in a detailed and authoritative way.[3] Yet since appraisals are being made all the time and general lessons are being derived from them, we may suggest some tentative conclusions as part of a process of historical interpretation that will go on for decades. The search for lessons naturally begins with the reasons for failure.

Four principal reasons for the failure in Vietnam emerge from the data and analyses available.

1. *The government (GVN), political system, and society of South Vietnam were too vulnerable to insurgency to preserve their independence by themselves or to be rescued by the United States, except at the cost of massive intervention and perhaps a U.S. protectorate.*

South Vietnam, created by the Geneva Accords of 1954, was a fractured society with no experience in self-government and no unifying traditions or sense of nationality, governed by urban elites remote from the villages and peasantry, dependent on an incompetent civil service and an untrustworthy army. The countryside was especially vulnerable to the culturally sensitive and well-organized adaptation of Mao's people's war led by Ho Chi Minh and General Giap, whose disciplined cadres promised liberation—from foreigners, corrupt bureaucrats, and poverty— under the rule of a new "mandate from heaven," while they systematically subverted and selectively terrorized the personnel on whom the GVN's effectiveness depended.

Nonetheless, contrary to the general assumption that the regime in South Vietnam would collapse, Prime Minister Ngo Dinh Diem succeeded for a while in restoring a modicum of authority and order. But while the Vietcong gained strength, Diem became increasingly isolated from the sources of political support as he fell back on a narrowing coterie of public officials, corrupt civil servants, repressive police, and venal local chieftains, thereby alienating the villagers and leaving them physically and politically vulnerable to disciplined, purposeful Vietminh cadres. Diem's political demise, however, was more than a personal failure in leadership. It reflected a system of governing that was based on the methods by which a military junta with no broad base of national support holds power.[4] For the GVN to have overcome its basic vulnerability to revolutionary war would have required it to transform this system of governing. But such a transformation would have undermined the authority of any regime that was likely to gain power. Transformation could not have been imposed by the United States, particularly in the midst of an insurgent war. No matter how dependent on U.S. aid the GVN might become, Washington was no more able to manipulate this aid to reform Diem's or Thieu's regimes than to reform Chiang Kai-shek's or Syngman Rhee's before. Therefore, U.S. technical and military assistance could not compensate for the deficiencies of government, and U.S. efforts to build a base of political cohesion and loyalty to the GVN in the countryside largely failed or had the opposite result of further weakening the authority of the regime.

Many Americans in Vietnam were conscious of the political and socioeconomic vulnerabilities of the Vietnamese, and the United States eventually instituted a multiplicity of programs that tried to overcome those vulnerabilities. But neither the strategic hamlet program (when the GVN carried the main military effort) nor the much larger pacification program (when the United States dominated the military effort) created the base of popular support and discipline that might have enabled either counterinsurgency or a war of attrition to win the *political* war in South Vietnam, even though both programs contributed to the near-defeat of North Vietnam militarily.

Winning the political war would have meant restoring the power and authority of a GVN that commanded the loyalty of the people in the countryside as well as in the cities. This was probably a task inherently beyond the capacity of any outside country. Therefore, although the strategic hamlet and the pacification programs, according to some supporters as well as critics, suffered from U.S. ignorance of the Vietnamese culture, poor organization, maladministration, bureaucratic indifference, lack of U.S. Army cooperation, and GVN obstruction, probably not even the most sophisticated and skillful efforts would have transformed South Vietnam into the kind of polity that could have mobilized popular support to win the protracted war of insurgency and establish a secure government. Under the indigenous political circumstances, it is unlikely that any improvements in counterinsurgency (such as those modeled on the operation in Malaya or those, like the Marine Corps' Combined Action Program, aimed at protecting the people more than at killing the enemy) or in regular military operations (such as those advocated by critics of the self-imposed limits on the war against North Vietnam in the North) could have won the war without massive infusions of U.S. armed forces and, perhaps, a U.S. military protectorate to preserve the fruits of victory. For the Democratic Republic of Vietnam (DRV), even if militarily devastated both in main battle-units (NVA) and Vietcong cadres—and most military observers believe that this was close to the situation from 1968 through 1971—could always have adjusted the tactics and scale of its operations in the South, waited for more propitious circumstances, restored its units and cadres, and continued the war until the U.S. got tired of trying to save the GVN from its inherent weakness.

2. *The American military were not properly trained, organized, or equipped to fight an insurgency; therefore, they transformed the war into an expanding conventional war, which,*

even though it virtually defeated North Vietnam militarily, the public was not willing to sustain.

Even if the political war against the guerrillas could have been won in a tolerable period of time by military operations more suited to supporting the people in the countryside, U.S. military forces were not prepared by doctrine or practice to fight that kind of war. Although the Kennedy administration regarded the war in Vietnam as a crucial test of the containment of wars of national liberation through counterinsurgency, the war in its decisive stage was predominantly a war of attrition fought by regular combat units. A case can be made for the proposition that the war of attrition was substantially won after the Tet offensive in February 1968. But in any case, simultaneously it was lost politically because Americans were not willing to sustain the human and economic costs of such a war when the prospect of political victory seemed so remote. Perhaps, if the U.S. role could have been confined to indirect assistance of a successful counterinsurgency, U.S. forces would have avoided the costs that induced the United States to withdraw and accept defeat. In fact, however, the weak and inept U.S. counterinsurgent efforts were doomed to fail. Instead of strengthening and refining these efforts, the United States introduced more and more regular troops in an expanding conventional war, and North Vietnam responded with infusions of its own regular forces (NVA) to create a large-scale conventional war along with its comprehensive guerrilla operations.[5]

If the basic reason for the failure of counterinsurgency was the political vulnerability of the GVN and the countryside to Ho Chi Minh's revolutionary war, an important subsidiary reason was the U.S. military establishment's lack of preparation for this kind of war. Despite the Kennedy administration's extensive introduction into the armed services of military and civic action programs, special units, and tactical training oriented toward counterinsurgency, these activities were added to the missions of regular combat units. They did not prepare U.S. armed forces to fight a large-scale guerrilla war. When the regular units became involved, counterinsurgent activities were overshadowed by the mode of fighting that U.S. armed forces had been trained, equipped, and organized to fight in Europe and Korea. This mode emphasized the most modern weapons, technical mobility, and concentration of firepower. Its objective was to find the enemy and kill as many as possible. To expect any other way of fighting would have presumed the creation of a large parallel counterinsurgency organization (which the Special Forces distinctly were not) or a radical transformation of the armed services at great cost to their morale and leadership and to their ability to fight regular warfare.

The armed forces of South Vietnam (ARVN) were equally unprepared for counterinsurgency, having been developed by the United States according to U.S. military doctrine and U.S. standards of modernization. Although many concessions were made to counterinsurgent techniques and tactics, the ARVN, like U.S. forces, were bound to fight the kind of conventional war they were primarily created to fight.

Consequently, when the United States decided to raise the level of military activity and introduce its own forces, following the failure of the strategic hamlet program and the demise of the Diem regime, the war became a strange amalgam of guerrilla warfare within an escalating conflict of regular combat forces and aerial bombing. In some respects the massive firepower and mechanized forces were ill adapted to the terrain, the tactics of the Vietcong, and the requirements of internal war. Therefore, military engagements constantly succeeded in seizing territory only to be followed by the return of the guerrillas when the troops moved on to the next engagement. A strategy aimed at killing as many of the enemy as possible, instead of protecting the people where they lived, was bound to conflict with the political mobilization of the countryside against the Vietcong. This was especially true because the Vietcong, operating under the cover of fortified villages, made it difficult to distinguish between civilians and combatants. Despite heavy casualties inflicted on DRV main battle units, enemy morale did not break and losses were replaced by infiltration and recruitment in the South, while the GVN failed to gain the allegiance of the people. At the same time, U.S. casualties were also heavy, and Hanoi knew that these casualties would be the decisive factor in achieving victory.

Nevertheless, the massive introduction of U.S. forces did exert a significant military effect. Technically, the B-52 bombing was particularly effective in defeating the NVA invasion of Easter 1972. The U.S./ARVN "search and destroy" campaign, starting in mid-1965, inflicted substantial costs on the NVA in big-unit combat as well as on the Vietcong in guerrilla operations. In desperation North Vietnam unleashed the risky Tet offensive of 1968, in which the Vietcong launched massive attacks against Saigon and other cities. As a result of Tet the Vietcong were devastated. The war reverted to guerrilla patterns with occasional surges of regular military action. When the Vietcong seemed in danger of losing their hold on the southern countryside in 1972, the NVA staged a conventional invasion of South Vietnam.

Waging the kind of war they were prepared to fight, U.S. forces in the South, with the help of aerial assaults against North Vietnam, clearly gained the upper hand in the conventional war. In the villages, too, Hanoi was losing the war. On the other hand, the GVN was not winning it. Alienation of the countryside from the Vietcong did not enable the GVN to gain a solid base of popular support. In any case, the decisive feature of the war was that Tet—as televised disproof of official optimism—convinced the U.S. public, many of the policymakers, and President Johnson himself that the objective of establishing a secure and independent South Vietnam could never be obtained militarily at an acceptable cost. When U.S. forces were steadily withdrawn in the process of "Vietnamization" and the Paris Agreements, ending U.S. involvement, were signed in January 1973, South Vietnam proved incapable of resisting the NVA invasion, and the U.S. was unwilling to reenter the war on a full scale to punish North Vietnamese violations of the agreements.[6]

3. *Incremental expansion of the war was inefficient militarily and fatal politically, but it does not necessarily follow that rapid escalation would have been politically feasible or successful.*

The gradual expansion of the scale of war by incremental infusions of U.S. forces was not in accord with the traditional doctrine and practice of U.S. armed forces. The traditional approach entailed a massive concentration of firepower against enemy forces in order to defeat them as quickly as possible. "Gradualism," as critics have described the incremental approach, resulted from (1) the fear that sudden and extensive escalation might lead to direct Chinese or Soviet intervention, (2) the reluctance of presidents either to lose the war without a greater effort or to fight it at any greater cost than necessary, and (3) the repeated underestimation of the effort that would be needed to win the war. Gradualism was, moreover, rationalized by the theory of limited war, which called for the restricted, flexible, controlled, proportionate use of force in order to persuade the adversary to terminate the war.

The result of gradualism in Vietnam was to permit the war to drag on at increasing cost and public opposition without the satisfaction of anticipating a clear-cut victory. North Vietnamese forces were given time to adjust the scale and tactics of their operations to each successive increment while enjoying the protection of geographical sanctuaries and target immunities that the United States imposed upon its own operations. Under these conditions, the longer the war lasted, the more successful Hanoi was in waging the political side of the war in South Vietnam and the United States—even though the North incurred increasing costs in military terms. Hanoi was determined to fight the war for total stakes: the incorporation of South Vietnam in a united Vietnam. To Hanoi, U.S. self-restraint confirmed the favorable balance of interests, which eventually would induce the United States to withdraw when the costs of war became disproportionate to U.S. interests.

Impelled to fight an expanding war of attrition but constrained to fight it incrementally and within cautiously imposed restrictions, some U.S. civilian officials looked to a more psychologically-oriented strategy of graduated, punitive escalation in order to persuade the adversary to terminate the war without having to defeat his forces. Frustrated by Hanoi's incursions in the South, in the spring of 1965 the United States launched ROLLING THUNDER—a highly selective, gradually intensified bombing of targets in North Vietnam on lists authorized by the president, intended to persuade Hanoi through "signals" and symbolic "bargaining" to accept reasonable limited terms of settlement under penalty of paying an increasing price for war.[7] Hanoi was not persuaded.[8] After three years the experiment in punitive bargaining was abandoned as a failure.

Perhaps the signals were not clear. Indeed, in response to public protests throughout the world, the United States stressed the purely military objectives of the bombing as though to deny their punitive function. Perhaps the escalation was not undertaken soon enough, by the right means, or in sufficiently big increments. Or perhaps the cost of the bombing in Hanoi's eyes was overestimated. More clearly, Hanoi simply was determined, after decades of persistence, to achieve its total national aim by any means, over any length of time, and at great cost; whereas the United States, with much more limited aims and interests, was in an inferior position in any contest of wills that entailed a military cost without a distinct military gain. Controlled escalation, though it inflicted heavy damage on Hanoi's war making capacity, did not sufficiently affect the balance of military capabilities to alter the balance of will and interests in the United States' favor. Restrictions on the bombing of industrial, supply, and transportation targets in a broad area around Haiphong and Hanoi were probably interpreted as confirmation of an inferior will to win. In any case, the difficulty of conducting a finely tuned campaign of controlled escalation against a belligerent with total aims in a civil war demonstrated the limits of gamesmanship and reciprocal self-restraint in the conduct of limited war.

In contrast to ROLLING THUNDER, the eleven-day bombing campaign undertaken in December 1972, called LINEBACKER, heavily damaged supply depots, transportation centers, port facilities, airfields, and military complexes and substantially reduced the flow of Chinese and Soviet supplies into North Vietnam and from North Vietnam to the South. Opponents of gradualism see a direct connection between the resulting effect on Hanoi's fighting power and its resumption of serious negotiation. More dubiously, some enthusiasts of airpower contend that an earlier bombing campaign like this could have brought the war to a successful conclusion in a matter of weeks in 1965 when North Vietnam's air defenses were still weak and its industrial capacity not yet dispersed. More credible is the conclusion that Secretary of Defense McNamara reached by late 1966: that to exert a radical impact on Hanoi's will would require a scale of bombing unacceptable to Americans and world opinion and would incur an excessive risk of Chinese intervention.

Nevertheless, impressed by the disadvantages and failures of gradualism, a number of retrospective critics of U.S. conduct of the war in Vietnam, like a few participants and observers at the time, have argued that the United States could and should have won the war by earlier and more extensive escalation. Or they have argued that if the United States were not prepared to incur the risk and political cost of sudden escalation, it should have stayed out of the war or withdrawn much earlier. There is a strong case, in retrospect, for the contention that sudden escalation, especially as applied against bases and lines of supply in the North and running through Laos, would have crippled the DRV's large-scale operations in the South without provoking direct Chinese or Soviet intervention.

All presidents ruled out using nuclear weapons, invading North Vietnam, destroying the dike system, and bombing the civilian population because the risk of Chinese intervention was too great; and these prohibitions were scarcely challenged, even by the military. The estimate of this risk, however, seems to have been based more on a misleading analogy to the Korean war than on a careful analysis of Peking's interests and capabilities in Indochina. President Johnson repeatedly opposed military recommendations to invade Cambodia and Laos and to bomb a variety of military and logistics targets and mine ports in the North, partly because of an expressed fear of Chinese intervention. Yet President Nixon authorized many of these actions without provoking either Chinese or Soviet counteraction. In reality, fears of Chinese intervention were reinforced by a number of other constraints—in particular, fear of domestic criticism and skepticism about the decisive effect of bombing and mining.[9] But probably the greatest constraint—and the basic reason for gradualism—was simply the tacit assumption that U.S. interests in the war did not warrant even a small risk of widening the war politically or, indeed, of enlarging it in any way beyond the minimum measures that seemed to be necessary to avoid defeat.

In any event, it is quite unlikely that massive escalation, whatever its immediate military effects, would have stopped the guerrilla warfare or enabled the GVN to overcome the political weaknesses that enabled such warfare to continue. Consequently, one must doubt that even an early military success through escalation would have enabled the United States to escape the frustrations and dissatisfactions of a protracted and ultimately lost war. The end would have been the same unless the threat of overwhelming the DRV and destroying its external supply lines had induced the PRC and the USSR to compel Hanoi to sue for peace under conditions that would have assured the GVN against renewed DRV military action. All the evidence of Hanoi's absolute determination to conquer and absorb the South refutes the likelihood of this outcome.

4. *The national interests at stake were not sufficiently compelling to Americans to have justified a scale and duration of*

combat necessary to win the war.

Whether by an intensified and protracted effort the United States could have won the war of attrition, whether it could have consolidated its post-Tet military advantage and established a lastingly independent South Vietnam, must remain unanswerable but doubtful speculations, given the historic persistence of the DRV and the political weakness of the GVN. It is clear, however, that both the intensity and the duration of the U.S. effort were diminished by popular disaffection with the war. This disaffection was not due to extraordinary material, human, economic, diplomatic, or moral costs alone. Although these costs somewhat exceeded those of the Korean war, the Korean war was also costly in lives, seemed equally frustrating, and was equally unpopular before the United States began winning.[10] The costs in Vietnam seemed excessive, in part, because they bore so little promise of victory. Also, despite the hyperbolic justifications of the U.S. effort as indispensable to the protection of the free world from Communist expansionism everywhere, neither the U.S. public nor its leaders really believed that the stakes in the Vietnam war were as important to U.S. security interests as in the Korean war and, of course, not remotely as vital as in World War II. By 1968 the overriding justification had become simply the maintenance of U.S. prestige, which especially meant the country's reputation for defending its allies under hardships. Indeed, the claim that the United States had honorably upheld its prestige eventually became a justification for withdrawing under the formula of "Vietnamization." Lacking any more tangible and convincing connection between the war and U.S. security, the costs of the war—particularly, the domestic ones—were bound to seem excessive.

Just as the costs of continuing the war came to seem excessive, the costs of waging it more intensively seemed to be unjustified. Consequently, U.S. leaders felt constrained to escalate the war on a piecemeal basis, reluctantly approving increased allocations of combat manpower in increments that seemed to be the minimum needed to avoid losing the war and the maximum the public would accept. When the increments caused a sharp rise in military spending in late 1965, President Johnson declined for three years to increase taxes in order to offset the resulting inflation. He also declined to call up reserves. And when his military advisors eventually recommended an increment of additional combat forces that could not be met without mobilizing the reserves, he decided to call a halt to the process and resign. To be sure, there were other reasons for not putting the nation on a wartime footing, but all of them could have been overcome if the objectives of the war had really been as compelling in tangible terms as its high-flown rationale implied.

Thus the Vietnam war posed acutely the issue that the Korean war had raised in a different form: How long and at what cost would the United States be willing to sustain a limited war? In Korea the issue was raised by those who urged escalation beyond the official geographical and weapons limitations rather than acceptance of stalemate. In Vietnam it was raised by those who preferred stalemate or defeat to escalation. It is significant, nonetheless, that in both cases the nation did fight a large-scale, protracted war within self-imposed restraints and in accordance with the theories of political limitation and proportionate force that are at the heart of limited-war strategy. One basic reason for the acceptance of self-imposed limitations under adverse military conditions is that in neither case did the interests at stake seem worth the risks of expanding the war. In this respect, cautious gradualism, as opposed to sudden and bold escalation in order to achieve the maximum military effect as soon as possible, seems intrinsic to the phenomenon of large-scale limited wars as the United States is disposed to fight them. Although the critics of gradualism who would opt for sudden escalation may be right on military grounds, they are almost certainly wrong on domestic political grounds.

The Limits of Lessons

If there are any lessons of general applicability that emerge from the U.S. experience in Vietnam, they are highly contingent, since so many of the military and political features of another local war are likely to be different or occur in different combinations. Moreover, the general lessons must be largely confined to the most salient characteristic of the war: that it was a large-scale, protracted local war in the Third World at a place of minor intrinsic national interest.

What should be the U.S. interest in intervening directly or indirectly in such a war? Is the lesson simply not knowingly to intervene in such a war under any conditions unless it can be won quickly or unless the Soviet Union would clearly exploit nonintervention to pose intrinsically serious threats to U.S. vital interests elsewhere? Perhaps. But can one know enough about the characteristics of such a war to apply such a general lesson? Considering the variety of conditions that might characterize such a war, one can prudently generalize only to the extent of saying that henceforth U.S. interests or the interests of other Western countries must not be assessed only in terms of a general commitment to stopping the expansion of communism or defeating Communist aggression. But intrinsic economic, political, and security interests and a sober estimate of both the prospect of a local Communist victory—or, one must now add, the victory of any unfriendly country or faction—and its consequences for the broader balance of power with the Soviet Union must also be taken into consideration. This lesson at least puts a greater burden of justification on the advocates of intervention, but it does not exclude all large-scale intervention and certainly not a variety of smaller, more controllable interventions.[11]

As for the feasibility of intervening successfully to support a government against an insurgency or to support one faction competing for power against others, it is difficult to estimate (before it is too late) the prospects for the government or a faction gaining a sufficient base of political support to be capable of being rescued. If the object of guerrilla war had that kind of support to begin with, there would be either no war or no need for much external help. The Vietnam example offers evidence that if indirect assistance is not sufficient, the direct participation of foreign troops is not likely to succeed either and could well make the situation worse. At least direct participation is not likely to succeed except at the cost of a protracted large-scale local war unless the opposing foreign conventional intervention is weak or nonexistent.

The Vietnam war seems to show that if the intervention of U.S. armed forces on a large scale is needed to prevent the defeat of a government or a faction engaged in an internal war, the United States will have great difficulty avoiding a war the cost and duration of which will not eventually become unacceptable domestically. Rapid and intense escalation probably will not avoid this situation at an acceptable risk of expanding the war, but gradualism may be equally costly and will tend to jeopardize the domestic base of support. In any case, graduated escalation is not likely to persuade the adversary to negotiate for peace except in proportion to the military effect it exerts (unless escalation persuades the adversary's nuclear protector that the risks of expanding the war are not worth running and the protector is in a position to persuade the protected to desist).

On the basis of the Vietnam experience one is tempted to conclude, as many military men do, that the United States—and the rule applies even more to its major allies—should not intervene in any kind of local war unless it can defeat the enemy and restore the status quo within a year or two by applying maximum military force within the geographical boundaries of the nation attacked. Some would add that U.S. armed forces should also refrain from intervening if the adversary is going to be permitted to enjoy adjacent sanctuaries outside the nation attacked. By implication, therefore, the United States should intervene only if it can attack such sanctuaries—unless, perhaps, this would create a clear and present danger of a direct encounter with Soviet forces. But even if these guidelines are sound, acting upon them presupposes advance knowledge about a complicated interaction of military and political factors that no one can predict or guarantee. Certainly the Vietnam experience tends to reinforce the arguments of the "winners" over the "limiters" among limited-war strategists. However, the nature and scope of the prudent limitations that even the "winners" would impose on efforts to defeat enemy forces will depend very much on such intangible factors as the importance of the interests at stake and the balance of interests between the United States and the Soviet Union, as well as upon such tangible factors as the local balance of military power and the proximity of Soviet forces. The difficulty of generalizing about these factors is illustrated by imagining the differences between the war in Vietnam and conceivable wars in the Near East.

Clearly, for those who accept the core of U.S. foreign policy and the prevailing broad concept of U.S. security interests, the lessons about limited-war strategy that can be derived from the Vietnam experience are so qualified that they are no more than cautionary items on a very long agenda of relevant considerations. At best these lessons serve as antidotes, if we need any, to the grand simplifications and ingenious stratagems of the Kennedy era.

In the short run, at least, it is somewhat easier to generalize about the lessons that U.S. statesmen, politicians, and military officers, rightly or wrongly, have in fact already derived from Vietnam[12]—although these generalizations do not go very far and they may not last very long. Perhaps the clearest and most enduring of these lessons concerns the place of unconventional war in the U.S. strategy of limited war. According to common wisdom, this lesson is simply that the United States must avoid fighting another such war with its own forces. Counterinsurgency remains a task for special forces, but it has ceased to be a doctrinal imperative or a practical concern for the regular armed forces. More ambiguously, the trauma of Vietnam has also affected the place of conventional local war in U.S. strategy in the Third World. (We shall deal with this in the last chapter.) It has apparently ruled out large-scale protracted local war, for example. Yet the essential rationale and doctrinal propositions of limited war, though surrounded by ambiguities, doubts, and controversies, manage to persist.

4
Post-Vietnam Refinements of Limited-War Strategy

The Growth of Soviet Military Power

Along with the effects of Vietnam on the U.S. approach to limited war, a number of other factors, independent of these effects, have been shaping strategic thought in the period since Vietnam. Among these factors are the accentuation and then the weakening of détente, the commitment to strategic arms control talks and agreements, the consolidation of strategic parity, the steady growth of Soviet military strength in both nuclear and conventional capabilities, the prospect of new weapons technology, the intensification of national and communal conflicts in the Third World, and the geographical expansion of Soviet and Cuban intervention abroad.

The formidable growth of Soviet military power since Vietnam, both absolutely and in comparison to U.S. military power,[1] impinges on every aspect of limited-war strategy. If this shift in the military balance had occurred in the late 1950s or 1960s the United States would be launched on a massive arms buildup in order to counter the basic military threat to U.S. security anticipated in limited-war theory. The fact that the actual U.S. response to this shift is far more limited, ambiguous, and diffused is indicative of the changes that have taken place in both international politics and U.S. foreign policy.

The Soviet Union not only has attained parity in strategic nuclear striking power but, contrary to the prevailing official and private expectations of the early 1960s, seems determined to achieve more than parity in order to be sure of achieving the most favorable war outcomes. At the same time, the Soviets have further enhanced their ability—already widely interpreted as superiority—to fight either a local or a theater-wide war in Europe by both conventional and nuclear means, and they have greatly improved their capacity to deny the West use of vital sealanes and to project military power by air and sea to distant lands. As significant as this shift in the military balance is the fact that, barring substantial increases in the U.S. defense effort, the shift will go on as the USSR continues to spend a consistently large and steady proportion of its GNP on defense.[2]

That this absolute and relative across the board increase of Soviet military strength has not created greater alarm or clearer policy direction in the West is not only the result of the Vietnam trauma. The Western reaction also reflects the more complicated relationship with the Soviet Union that has developed and the more complex international environment within which that relationship must be assessed. Fundamentally, it signifies the infusion of limited-war thinking with a more sophisticated— or at least more complicated—approach to the effect of military capabilities on political relationships.

The resulting uncertainties and ambiguities in the U.S. response to the Soviet military buildup have been greatest in applying limited-war strategy to the containment of the Soviet presence and influence in the Third World, where the nature of U.S. security interests, the extent of the Soviet threat, and the utility of U.S. military power are most in question. But even with respect to the central strategic balance and Western Europe, where the old political assumptions largely prevail, some of the original inferences about the significance of the military balance are in doubt. In particular, inferences about Soviet intentions are in doubt.

As at the onset of the cold war, the questions of Soviet intentions—then raised by Soviet behavior in Eastern Europe and the Mediterranean area—can now be posed in sweeping terms. Is the steady Soviet military buildup part of a grand geo-political design of expansion? Does it spring from a plan to destroy the outposts of democratic capitalism piecemeal prior to overwhelming the eroded core (the United States, its West European allies, and Japan)? Is the buildup now the substructure of an ascendant Soviet imperial drive that is inexorably displacing the shrinking empire of Western control and influence—just as the Soviets were seen to be threatening to fill the "power vacuum" in Western Europe in the late 1940s? Or does this buildup merely manifest the ceaseless pursuit of self-defense by a country with historically insecure boundaries, now threatened by restive and unreliable allies to the west, a hostile China to the east, and an encircling belt of U.S. clients and bases backed by the undisputed technological and industrial primacy of the United States in alliance with the world's most advanced economic powers? Does the Soviet pursuit of military strength spring more from the power and bureaucratic inertia of its military-industrial establishment than from offensive designs?

To question the significance of Soviet military power in these abstract terms is not likely to be helpful since the collective motives of any government are complex and difficult to divine and since quite different actions may follow from a particular motive or set of motives. More useful, if still inconclusive, is to relate Soviet military power to conceptions of national security and interests, deep-rooted images of international reality, historic patterns of behavior, certain propensities toward the use of military power, and to capabilities and opportunities to carry out these propensities. For this reason U.S. policy-makers came to rely upon a somewhat more complicated and subtle set of assumptions about the sources of Soviet conduct, as formulated most notably by George Kennan, than could be subsumed under the concept of "intentions."

We shall return to this question of the significance of the Soviet military buildup in the final chapter, which reassesses underlying assumptions about the sources of Soviet conduct and the role of containment in U.S. foreign policy. Suffice it to note here that the impact of Soviet military capabilities on limited-war strategy is now, as in the 1950s, as much a function of premises about U.S. interests as of perceptions about Soviet intentions. The strategy of limited war remains the creature of the foreign policy, indeed the whole approach to the outside world, that gave it birth.

The Doctrine of Limited Strategic War Revived

Despite the latent impact of the Vietnam experience on U.S. foreign policy and therefore on U.S. military strategy, the initial elaborations of limited-war strategy displayed more continuity than change. The first post-Vietnam reactivation of limited-war strategy was Secretary of Defense James R. Schlesinger's 1974 promulgation of a new policy toward the employment of strategic nuclear weapons in a central war.[3] The rationale, military objectives, and political functions of this strategy were the same as in the strategies of limited counterforce options and city avoidance formulated in the 1960s. But Schlesinger was determined to translate theory into effective operational plans for implementing a range of limited strategic responses to a variety of contingencies—principally, those that might arise from conflicts in Europe.

The impressive modernization and expansion of the Soviet intercontinental striking force in the years following the Cuban missile crisis provided an added incentive for the implementation of a strategy of limited nuclear exchanges. The Soviet achievement of a rough parity of strategic nuclear capabilities, only hypothetical in the 1960s, became the officially acknowledged basis of the SALT I agreement and of continuing negotiations to restrict the superpowers' strategic weapons programs.[4] Given parity in the superpowers' capacity to destroy each other (no matter which one struck first), a strategy of unlimited nuclear retaliation made less sense than ever to those who took seriously the prospect of actually having to fight a strategic nuclear war and did not simply rely on the deterrent effect of a hypothetical catastrophe. The development of more accurate strategic weapons, more flexible targeting, and more reliable C³ systems provided a new technical opportunity to hold open the option of making a strategic nuclear exchange a rational instrument of policy instead of an act of national suicide.

In important respects Secretary of Defense Schlesinger started a process of translating the theory of limited strategic nuclear options into operational reality backed by a government consensus. Counterforce capabilities still fall far short of the hypothetical requirements of such options. The United States and its allies must still make political decisions concerning specific limitations, and solve practical problems related to detailed contingency planning, supporting weapons, and C³ systems. Nevertheless, the process of implementing a strategy of limited nuclear options in central war seems likely to continue. Expectations about the utility of such a strategy as an instrument of U.S. policy, however, will remain minimal, in marked contrast to the enthusiasm that accompanied the strategy's first private and official pronouncements in the 1960s.[5] This moderation of expectations was apparent in the public debate that followed Schlesinger's announcement.

In this debate the critics voiced the same concerns as before: that a strategy of limited nuclear war is unworkable, provocative, and destabilizing and will stimulate the arms race and undermine the prospects of a strategic arms limitation treaty.[6] In response to these criticisms Secretary of Defense Schlesinger made modest claims for the strategy of limited strategic nuclear options. For the nuclear deterrent to conventional aggression in Europe the United States would still rely first on tactical nuclear weapons. The strategy of limited strategic nuclear options, by enhancing the credibility of nuclear retaliation, would make the resort to nuclear war less, not more, likely. The strategy was intended simply to hold open the possibility of relating strategic nuclear exchanges to rational political objectives, in whatever form or contingency the exchanges might originate, not to make the resort to nuclear war more attractive. Counterforce capabilities were not intended to disarm the adversary and could not significantly limit damage unless the number of nuclear exchanges were strictly limited. Finally, a strategy of limited nuclear exchanges would not necessarily affect the size of strategic forces.

Again, in Europe the strategy of limited central war was met largely with apathy, bewilderment, skepticism, or suspicion, except among a few defense experts and officials, mostly in Germany. However, there was no disposition to oppose the latest example of U.S. strategic innovation officially, except in France. But again, Moscow condemned the strategy, and, despite achievement of a markedly less vulnerable strategic force and a more effective counterforce capability, the Soviets showed no signs of having modified their emphasis on a strategy of war-fighting and war-survival intended to both disarm and devastate the adversary with a sudden massive concentration of firepower. Although the Soviet Union now possesses the capability to implement a variety of limited strategic nuclear options, its spokesmen show not the slightest inclination to adopt concepts of controlled escalation, intrawar bargaining, and the like.[7] This stance does not necessarily invalidate U.S. efforts to apply these concepts to control strategic nuclear war, but it certainly dampens expectations that the concepts will be implemented in an actual confrontation.

The utility of limited strategic war as a means of controlling the process of escalation following the resort to nuclear weapons against conventional aggression is undermined, in any case, by the growing Soviet counterforce capability, which according to most experts will pose an almost total threat to U.S. silo-housed ICBMs by the mid-1980s. Consequently, even if the Soviets were willing to limit strategic nuclear exchanges, the prospect of a Soviet Union with equal or superior strategic nuclear capability (using almost any measure) seems destined to provide Moscow, not Washington, with the theoretical advantage (according to U.S. logic) in waging controlled strategic war.[8]

Limited-War Strategy in Europe

The application of limited-war strategy to Europe, as to the U.S.-USSR nuclear balance, reflected the basic continuity of U.S. foreign policy and strategic concepts. In the late 1970s a number of developments merged to revive the efforts of analysts and governments to cope with the familiar strategic problems of NATO: the codification of strategic parity in the SALT agreement and negotiations; the continued absolute and relative growth of the Soviet nuclear striking force; the concomitant modernization and expansion of Soviet forces in Europe, the further development of more accurate, flexible, and mobile conventional as well as nuclear weapons technology; the persistence of pressures to hold down manpower expenditures in defense budgets; and the end of the distractions of Vietnam. NATO also became the site of the first significant effort to implement limited-war strategy with new forces and weapons. But the basic strategic issues underlying this renewed effort remained the same, and neither new tactics nor new technology seemed likely to resolve them.

The prevailing NATO strategy in the 1970s remained as expressed in MC 14/3 and supported by the "NATO Triad" of conventional, theater nuclear, and strategic forces. Within the bounds of this strategy the allies have never been more solidly committed, in theory and declaration, to a strategy of flexible and controlled response and to the prerequisite of raising the nuclear threshold, but in the mid-1970s there was no commensurate increase of conventional capabilities. Indeed, the significant change in European military capabilities occurred not in NATO but in the Warsaw Pact, where the modernization and full manning of Soviet divisions since the mid-1960s compounded the projected difficulty of NATO's achieving a forward defense.[9]

Soviet conventional forces, many now fear, could launch a blitzkrieg without mobilizing and with only a few days' warning instead of the twenty-three- to thirty-day mobilization posited in NATO plans.[10] Using only conventional weapons, these forces might occupy much of Germany and leave NATO in the predicament of launching a counteroffensive with nuclear weapons, which would surely devastate Germany. At the same time, the great advance in Soviet TNW would deter NATO from responding with battlefield nuclear weapons, while the Soviet Union's greatly augmented strategic nuclear striking power would deter the United States from turning a theater war into central war. Such a conventional blitzkrieg would be consistent with Soviet military doctrine and also with the facts of geography and politics, in that NATO's force ratio would become more advantageous in thirty days or more with U.S. mobilization and reinforcements, and a quick occupation of German territory could provide the Soviets with a favorable basis for negotiating a settlement before the war escalated.

The proper response to this danger, most strategists believe, is to build up NATO's capability for forward conventional defense. Indeed, in light of the relative advantage that Soviet forces may now enjoy in theater nuclear war and the parity they have achieved in strategic capabilities, NATO's best strategy could be conventional war, while the Warsaw Pact has the advantage in initiating nuclear war if its objectives are not achieved by conventional means. But achieving an effective forward defense will require money, a host of remedies for specific deficiencies, and perhaps some basic structural reforms.

A few strategists, convinced that the inadequacy of NATO's forward conventional defense is inherent in the facts of geography and relative military resources, have argued for repulsing a Warsaw Pact invasion at the border with the early use of low-yield, discriminating TNW.[11] But the explicit revival of the strategy of substituting TNW for conventional responses no longer finds much favor in the absence of any new reason, other than the availability of more discriminating nuclear weapons, to believe that a tactical nuclear war could either be significantly limited or won at a reasonable cost. Although Soviet military doctrine and policies can now be construed to support the contingency of a theater nuclear war excluding the Soviet Union and the United States from the combat zone, there is no reason to think that Soviet forces, still oriented toward a blitzkrieg offensive, would employ TNW for any objectives other than defeating the adversary as quickly and thoroughly as possible or that NATO could win such a war without incurring enormous devastation of allied territory.[12]

A more optimistic view of the conventional balance sees the overall quantitative war-fighting capabilities of NATO and the Warsaw Pact as fairly equal, doubts the reliability of East European contingents, and questions the plausibility of the blitzkrieg scenario from the standpoint of Soviet interests and the deployment of Soviet forces. Moreover, in this view, creating the kind of force that could fend off such a blitzkrieg would cost far more than NATO countries are willing to spend and could be offset by the deployment of more Soviet forces near the forward line. The conclusion drawn from this view is not that the nuclear threshold should be lowered—the time for this logic has passed—but that the West must continue to seek an arms control agreement that will create a more stable military balance through mutual balanced force reductions (MBFR).[13] Although hopes for solving NATO's military problems through MBFR seem dim, the fear of further worsening this prospect has sometimes reinforced arguments against substantial expenditures for improving NATO's military posture. Nonetheless, for those who believe that modest expenditures can achieve an adequate balance of war-fighting capabilities there was cause for optimism in the agreement of NATO members in May 1977, to increase defense expenditures for NATO by 3 percent.

Whether optimistic or not about the prospect of increasing conventional forward defense capabilities in Europe, the United States is bound to stress the priority of this objective, since its inhibitions against using nuclear weapons first are by now so deeply entrenched.[14] Although the government does not dare renounce nuclear first-use for fear of undermining deterrence and allied confidence, the principal function of TNW in operational reality has become the deterrence of, and response to, Soviet first-use of TNW. To support this function with a flexible and controlled nuclear response Secretary of Defense Schlesinger began the first serious effort to make limited nuclear options operationally feasible by restructuring NATO forces, revising targeting plans, and bringing nuclear weapons under more effective command and control procedures. The resulting strategy of controlled escalation, however, depended heavily on some conditions that no longer existed—particularly, U.S. strategic nuclear superiority and NATO superiority at virtually every level of escalation.

Confronted with the new emphasis on the old problem of achieving an effective forward conventional defense of Germany at an acceptable cost in the face of increasing Soviet conventional and nuclear strength, Western defense analysts and officials have turned once again to technological innovations to alleviate the problem. However, in contrast to the 1950s, this time innovations are being sought within the context of the strategy of flexible and controlled response and with no promise of either a technical or tactical solution to the strategic predicament. Precision guided munitions (PGMs), new guided delivery vehicles (particularly cruise missiles), and improved C^3 promise to give conventional forces greater mobile firepower, accuracy at long range, concealment and dispersal, and flexibility in the selection of targets, combined with the destruction of targets at long range and the minimization of collateral damage.[15]

Optimistic assessments anticipate that this technology will enhance NATO's conventional defense and reduce reliance on TNW while facilitating the controlled use of force for specific political effects. However, others point to certain technical weaknesses of PGMs, the vulnerability of C^3 to countermeasures, and the need for new tactics and organization to exploit the new technology effectively. Some analysts calculate that PGMs will accelerate the rate of destruction and of weapons consumption and therefore leave less time for pausing to bargain in a local war; that Soviet countermeasures such as area bombing and concentration of destruction on rear-area support facilities will nullify the PGMs' enhancement of controlled limitations; and that Soviet PGMs could facilitate an attack in Europe by enhancing the precise destruction of bases, supplies, ports, and industry at long range.

On balance, the new technology seems to favor a strategy of flexible and controlled response, but it does not promise relief from the problem of achieving an effective forward defense at a politically acceptable cost. Moreover, like TNW, the new conventional military technology introduces new uncertainties into limited-war strategy because it expands the range of hypothetical outcomes of warfare in Europe in the absence of any further empirical basis for guessing the real consequences.[16]

Greater strategic implications may follow from NATO's prospective adoption of long-range cruise missiles with optional conventional or nuclear warheads. These weapons hypothetically offer NATO the opportunity to destroy critical military targets, such as radar sites and transportation centers, deep in Eastern Europe and in the Soviet Union itself with conventional instead of nuclear warheads. Consequently, they might enhance local denial capabilities and raise the nuclear threshold in theater and even central war. The promise of this military effect, however, is clouded by speculations about subsidiary political effects. By making conventional strikes at the Soviet Union more attractive might not cruise missiles, in reality, more quickly provoke a Soviet nuclear response, possibly in a preemptive attack? And would they not tend to break down the distinction between nuclear and conventional war by virtue of their dual capability? On the other hand, if cruise missiles succeed in raising the level of conventional resistance, might they not reduce the credibility of nuclear escalation and so diminish deterrence in West European eyes? Or would they enhance deterrence and increase allied control over the scope of the war by providing allied battlefield commanders with a means of striking at Soviet targets without exclusive U.S. authorization? Therefore, might cruise missiles not create a new European interest in raising the nuclear threshold?

Considering the steady rise of nuclear inhibitions and the search for technology that will raise the level of effective conventional resistance, the arguments in favor of long-range cruise missiles based in Europe will probably carry the day unless they are rejected on the grounds that cruise missiles would stimulate the arms race and impede the achievement of a strategic arms limitation treaty and MBFR.[17] Their real effect on deterrence, however, will be impossible to measure, and their effect on NATO's war-fighting capability will be only hypothetical, since neither objective, one hopes, will be subject to an empirical test.

The same logic—or psychology—that favors raising the nuclear threshold with more precise and flexibly controlled conventional weapons also favors limiting nuclear war with more precise, flexible, and controllable nuclear weapons once the threshold is crossed—except that some fear the new nuclear weapons may obscure the threshold itself. Two kinds of small-yield, so-called "mini-nukes"—one, based on fission, with reduced blast and radiation; the other, based on fusion, with reduced blast and enhanced short-term radiation (popularly known as the "neutron bomb")—might exploit the greater military effect of nuclear weapons with less collateral damage and thereby enhance the utility and political acceptability of TNW as denial forces while introducing new small steps on the escalation ladder—assuming that the Soviet Union would observe compatible limitations. These weapons would not, however, overcome the familiar problems inherent in a nuclear first-use strategy and would compound these problems if mini-nukes were to be considered a substitute for an enhanced conventional response.[18] Mini-nukes make the most sense, some military commanders and defense officials have plausibly argued, as substitutes for the bulk of the 7000 large-yield TNW that had accumulated in Europe by the mid-1960s—many in vulnerable locations, on quick reaction alert, and under uncertain command and control—and as part of a revised NATO military posture to get more conventional power for existing defense expenditures.[19] So far, however, the efforts of some U.S. defense officials since the mid-1960s to reduce substantially the number of TNW in Europe have encountered strong resistance among the allies who fear any such move will weaken the deterrent effect of TNW and lead to the decoupling of TNW from the U.S. strategic force.

Regardless of the strategic issues and political complications raised by new conventional and nuclear weapons, the prospect is that NATO will gradually assimilate them as it has assimilated new weapons in the past. Their utility for limited warfare, however, will depend centrally on tactical doctrines, military missions, and military organization and procedures—notoriously much slower to change. No new technology could have as great an effect on NATO's capacity to implement a strategy of flexible and controlled response as success in overcoming a number of structural deficiencies: force plans and military organization preoccupied with a war of attrition at the expense of maneuver, the lack of standardization (or, more broadly, "interoperability") of allied weapons and logistics, the illogical deployment of national forces, and the bloated size of NATO divisions.[20]

In any event, all these much-studied issues may be less urgent than those arising from political developments on NATO's southern flank. Understandably, the reconsideration of familiar strategic issues in terms of new military technology has taken place almost exclusively with respect to the central front in Europe because, for political reasons, this has been the focus of NATO's military concern from the beginning. It is ironic that this focus should have so dominated the 1970s, a period when for political reasons the threat to the central front is generally estimated to have subsided to an unprecedented low; whereas disturbing political changes along the Mediterranean flank of Europe may be confronting NATO with the greatest potential threats to cohesion and strength since its founding.

The reactivation of the old conflict between Greece and Turkey by controversies over the control of Cyprus and petroleum rights in the Aegean, the concomitant loosening of Greek and

Turkish ties to NATO and the United States, the possibility that the death of Tito will lead to national strife in Yugoslavia and appeals for outside aid, the ascendance of Communist parties to positions of influence and power in countries with serious economic and social problems (notably, Portugal and Italy), the possibly rising influence in several European countries of leftist groups that are likely to be more actively hostile to NATO and the status of U.S. forces in NATO than the Communist parties, the latent danger that Soviet suppression of organized East European dissidence might spill over the not-so-Iron Curtain—these developments present a far more diversified and also divisive set of threats of direct and indirect Soviet military intervention than the NATO countries have faced before. They call for a more diversified and politically discriminating set of military responses, with implications for conventional weapons systems, rules of engagement, the stationing of forces, naval deployments, bases, and institutional arrangements for bilateral and multilateral military action.[21] Whether these implications involve military strategy or just military tactics and organization is perhaps a matter of definition, but they certainly involve significant problems of implementing limited-war strategy that the NATO countries have only begun to consider.

Limited-War Strategy in the Third World

The Political Premises Revised

In contrast to the strategies of limited central war and limited local or theater war in Europe, there has been a notable absence in the 1970s of new tactical or technical concerns or even of the revival or reappraisal of old strategic concerns with respect to limited-war strategy in the Third World. It is as though the trauma of Vietnam had suspended creative thought in this area. Where foreign policy is most in doubt military strategy is least active.

The most notable developments in military thought about Third World contingencies have been the virtual disappearance of two features of limited-war strategy that emerged in the wake of the Korean war: reliance on counterinsurgency as a response to wars of national liberation (or, for that matter, any other kind of war) and reliance on tactical nuclear strikes as a response to direct Chinese or Soviet military intervention. The first feature was a victim of the no-more-Vietnams sentiment and the discovery of the formidable obstacles to successful U.S. intervention in internal wars. The second declined in favor because of the growing popular and material constraints against initiating the use of nuclear weapons, except perhaps in vital strategic areas, and the growing perception, reinforced by the Vietnam war, that neither the Soviet Union nor China is at all likely to resort to large-scale direct intervention anyway.

The problems of applying the general rationale of limited-war strategy to central war and to local war in Europe arise from old issues and new technology that transcend the impact of the Vietnam war. The problems of applying limited-war strategy outside the European theater, where the strategy received its greatest official impetus in the Kennedy period, arise because the Vietnam experience has raised fundamental questions, first, about the political premises that underlay the Kennedy-approved strategy of counter-insurgency as an instrument of containment and, more broadly, about the premises behind the whole rationale of direct U.S. armed intervention by any means in local wars in the Third World. The premises behind U.S. intervention have an operational military dimension; but basically they concern the nature of U.S. security interests, the threats to these interests, and the intrinsic capability of U.S. armed forces to cope with them. In contrast to the 1960s, each of these premises has been downgraded and qualified.

All observers of trends in U.S. foreign policy note that the prevailing conception of U.S. security interests has become more selective. Despite the rising concern in the United States about Soviet intervention in Africa and elsewhere, the chain-of-aggression (or falling dominoes) thesis in the post-Vietnam outlook no longer automatically justifies U.S. military intervention in behalf of Third World countries threatened with a local Communist takeover.[1] The tendency now is to evaluate the importance of U.S. security interests ad hoc, according to the particular geographical and political conditions that surround a perceived Soviet threat.

An equally marked change of outlook is the shift from the confidence of the 1960s in U.S. capacity to cope with peripheral wars to the present prevailing doubts about the ability of the United States to intervene effectively in any large-scale local wars in the Third World. This shift is most noticeable in the executive branch and the armed services, where diminished confidence in the government's ability to intervene at a cost and duration that Congress and the public will support is apparent.

No less significant but perhaps more subject to change with changing circumstances, the prevailing estimate of the nature and intensity of the Communist threat of expansion in the Third World has been downgraded. If Americans perceived the threat of Communist expansion now as they saw it in the 1960s, the government would be preparing for military intervention, not worrying about how to avoid it. But the fear of Chinese aggression, which was so intense after the Korean war and at the onset of U.S. involvement in Vietnam, has almost vanished since the Nixon-Kissinger rapprochement put U.S.-PRC relations on the road to normalization. Moreover, the prevailing estimate of the threat of Soviet armed intervention and of the Soviet ability to maintain and capitalize upon positions of influence in the Third World has also diminished significantly.

Many international developments account for this perceived devaluation of the Communist threat: the development of détente following a set of negotiations and agreements with the Soviet Union, the rapprochement with Peking, the perpetuation of the Sino-Soviet split, the continuing fragmentation of Communist parties in the world, Soviet political reverses in Egypt and other "client" states, the dissolution of colonial holdings susceptible to wars of national liberation, the declining appeal of Soviet leadership on ideological grounds, the pragmatism and independence of Third World countries, and the cross-cutting and shifting configurations of power and interests in Africa and other parts of the Third World. But the catalytic cause for the devaluation of the Communist threat is simply the shock the agonies of the Vietnam war administered to all the premises of containment that were held responsible for U.S. intervention.

The Security Threat Revived

Nevertheless, it would be misleading to conclude that the premises of the U.S. strategy of limited war in the Third World have eroded entirely. Some key premises endure. The general framework and most of the elements of the U.S. security outlook remain in force, and there are plenty of international developments to sustain and even accentuate or enlarge that outlook. It is significant that U.S. leaders continue to define U.S. security interests broadly in terms of preserving a tolerable degree of international order—not only against direct Soviet intervention but also against indigenous armed conflicts that threaten U.S. allies, citizens, and vital material interests. The importance of international order as an element of the U.S. conception of security is also enhanced by the common assumption that the world continues to shrink in real political space while growing more interdependent economically, ecologically, politically, and militarily. The scope of U.S. concern about international order, moreover, is enlarged by new threats not directly related to U.S.-Soviet competition: nuclear proliferation; international terrorism; OPEC decisions on oil prices and supply; the fusion of racial, tribal, and ethnic animosity with national rivalries in the Third World; the new possibility that even small countries in the nonindustrial world may constrict U.S. commerce, access to important resources, and the unhampered use of sealanes and straits for commercial and military use; the distinct probability that small and medium powers will increasingly seek the military assistance of the United States, the Soviet Union, and the former colonial states of Europe in support of their interests in local conflicts.

Indeed, as a general threat to international stability, the diffusion of modern military capabilities among middle-range powers and the increasing number of militarily significant independent actors affecting the international system could be more troublesome to U.S. interests than all the wars of national liberation in the 1960s. Cuba's program of foreign military assistance, including direct combat support in Africa and other distant parts of the world, demonstrates the historically unprecedented ambition and ability of even a less-than-middle-range power to project its military power abroad, albeit with indispensable Soviet material and political support. Although

Cuban imperialism arises from unique domestic roots in the Castro revolution,[2] its continued success could be a disruptive example of small-power adventurism to others. But quite apart from this example, the number of states that are potentially and actually engaged in significant armed conflicts with their neighbors has greatly increased in the last decade, most dramatically in Africa.

Along with these systemic factors foreboding international disorder, the accentuation of some more specific threats to the United States' familiar view of its security interests tends to reactivate cold war attitudes. Containment of Soviet power and influence is still seen to be the most important objective of U.S. policy, since the USSR is by all odds the greatest potential threat to U.S. security. Two developments now seem to increase this threat: (1) Soviet naval and air capacity to project forces overseas and impede the projection of U.S. forces has expanded. (2) Moscow is evidently determined to advance Soviet access to and influence in the troubled Third World, particularly Africa, through arms transfers, military advisers, military alliances (as in South Yemen, Ethiopia, Afghanistan, and Vietnam), and Cuban forces and military advisers. These two developments remind Americans that, where Soviet opportunities for projecting military power abroad appear, there may still be a military dimension to containment in peripheral areas.[3]

In Southeast Asia the Soviet capacity to exploit regional conflicts in the aftermath of U.S. withdrawal is, for the time being, contained by the proximity of China and an uneasy balance of power in the peninsula, with the USSR and the PRC backing opposing sides. But the success of Soviet-backed, historically expansionist Vietnam in overwhelming Laos and Cambodia and the Chinese "punitive" invasion of Vietnam indicate that the indigenous regional balance is inherently unstable and that at least three great powers—the USSR, the PRC, and the U.S.—have a stake in the future of this balance that could conceivably lead to armed confrontations.

In Africa neither China nor any indigenous balance restrains the exploitation of regional conflicts; and only the French, among the keepers of the former colonial order, maintain an active security role. Moscow's projection of Soviet power and presence beyond its European perimeter, with the cover of political legitimacy lent by African appeals for the defense of historic boundaries and the achievement of black majority rule, make Soviet ambitions in Africa considerably more formidable than in the 1960s. The Soviet Union's announced determination to support "socialist," "anticolonialist," and "anti-imperialist" forces as a moral and historic duty is, of course, no surprise. There is also nothing new in Soviet opportunistic extension of support to or withdrawal of support from states without regard to ideology or in Soviet insistence that coexistence and détente are consistent with—indeed, are promoted by—military aid to (and direct military involvement in the affairs of) emerging nations in order to eliminate "racism and colonialism."[4] What is new is the Soviet willingness and ability to project arms and combat units to nonadjacent areas, as in the war between Ethiopia and Somalia (first to Somalia and then to Ethiopia), where neither material Soviet interests, security, or commitments are at stake.[5]

Ironically, just when the feared threat of expanding Soviet influence in the Third World becomes more realistic, the United States is far more inhibited from countering it. The ultimate irony is that, conscience stricken by the U.S. intervention in Vietnam, many Americans are morally disarmed from reacting to Soviet adventures in Africa by a Vietnam-like vision of the United States again taking the role of an international policeman defending the independence of states and the integrity of territorial boundaries. Nevertheless, if present trends in the expansion of Soviet influence and intervention continue, U.S. inhibitions must arise less from depreciation of the Soviet threat than from the inability to find the political conditions for doing anything to counter that threat. For it is clear that the U.S. government still regards local wars, revolutions, and civil disturbances in distant parts of the world as potentially dangerous to U.S. security, either because these conflicts might invite Soviet exploitation or because they might indirectly impinge on U.S. economic and political interests. The media, moreover, bring daily evidence to the general public of a variety of violent disorders in the world, ranging from terrorism to limited and full-scale wars: ethnic, tribal, and other kinds of communal conflicts; coups, insurrections, and civil wars; interstate raids, border clashes, and invasions; guerrilla and regular warfare. Not all of these disorders, of course, impinge on intrinsic U.S. material interests or pose the danger of Soviet intervention. But, together with the enhanced Soviet military and political capacity to exploit them, they constitute an unprecedented concentration of the kind of disturbances in the international environment that have embroiled the United States in the past. The post-Vietnam inhibitions against involvement seem to insulate the U.S. from these disorders at present, but these inhibitions may erode if disorders of the Third World continue to provide opportunities for Soviet intervention.

Africa, until recently the least militarized of continents, seems ripe for the greatest proliferation of local wars in the whole postwar period of decolonization and new nationhood—wars that could involve the participation of extracontinental powers with arms and military units. The military weakness and insecurity of African states; the divisive effects of increasingly violent national, ethnic, and racial conflicts; and the reluctance of the United States and the former colonial powers to be on the "wrong" side of anticolonial on antiwhite passions give the Soviets and Cubans attractive opportunities to achieve new positions of influence (for whatever combination of ideological or strategic reasons) and to erode Western positions of influence through limited forms of military intervention at seemingly low costs and risks.[6] Under these conditions the United States lacks the domestic or international political base for counterintervention, except as frustrated mediator and peacemaker. The Soviet Union and Cuba, on the other hand, can interject arms and troops with impunity and even with approval in African eyes. Yet the United States is no less anxious now than before Vietnam to avoid giving Moscow license to fish in troubled waters without fear of opposition. If historical examples are relevant, one might expect the African situation to lead to a direct or indirect U.S.-USSR encounter, following from Moscow's underestimation of Washington's will to resist, Washington's sudden decision that the line must finally be drawn, and the inability of either to predict or control indigenous conflicts.

On the other hand, the Soviet threat may remain safely below the threshold of provoking or enabling U.S. military counterintervention. It is not easy to see what *lasting* assets Moscow could acquire from Africa that would threaten U.S. vital interests or why Moscow should pursue them incautiously.[7] Perhaps the USSR seeks naval bases and staging areas; the alliance of a few "socialist" regimes for ideological and anti-Chinese reasons; the aggravation of indigenous national and racial animosities that will obstruct Western access and influence; and more doubtfully, in the long run, the provocation and support of a massive race war against South Africa. But the prospect of Moscow managing to gain a paramountcy in Africa such that the USSR would be willing and able to exploit raw materials against the West and threaten vital sealanes around the continent, even if it had the incentive and were willing to run the risks, seems farfetched.

More disturbing from the standpoint of U.S. military planning may be the prospect of local conflicts in parts of the Third World that are intrinsically more important than Africa; far more important than Vietnam for economic, political, and strategic reasons; and also closer to the central bases of Soviet power. The renewal of Arab-Israeli warfare or a spreading revolution of radical or antimodernist forces in the Near East could confront the United States and its NATO allies with the reintroduction of Soviet influence—perhaps even a Soviet presence in the area—or, more likely, the disruption of oil supplies by local turmoil or embargo. An indigenous Middle East conflict or revolution might invite Soviet covert intervention or military pressure that would compel more than a diplomatic response from the United States because of U.S. interests and commitments. The collapse of the shah's regime in the winter of 1978-1979 showed how precarious has been the U.S. reliance on Iran as a proxy to secure a favorable international order in an area of vital economic and strategic interest. The repercussions of this sudden change in the regional balance of power, combined with Soviet alliances with Afghanistan, South Yemen, and Ethiopia, were bound to give Saudi Arabia and other moderate, friendly Arab regimes a sense of encirclement and insecurity that the United States could only offset with a successful demonstration of U.S. military power in behalf of its general diplomatic strategy in the region.[8]

The security of South Korea is as crucial to the stability of the geopolitically vital Northeast Asian area as Iran's security is to the Middle East. In Korea the relative growth of North Korean military strength and the prospective withdrawal of remaining U.S. forces from the South might upset the balance of power in the area, as the U.S. intervention and withdrawal has evidently done in Indochina. In Korea the convergence of conflicting great-power interests raises the prospect of external involvement in a local war and places a new premium on U.S. deterrence of Soviet (and perhaps Chinese) intervention.

In contingencies like these, the domestic and international political constraints against U.S. armed intervention that have become so conspicuous since the Vietnam war would not necessarily prevail. As the Korean war showed, the fact that Americans have difficulty imagining armed intervention in distant places is no assurance that the U.S. government will find an acceptable alternative to intervention if an unforeseen crisis occurs. To be sure, U.S. statesmen and military leaders show a greater disposition to stay out of local conflicts even when the contestants (as in Africa) appeal for arms against self-styled Marxist regimes supported by Soviet and Cuban arms. Congress's cut-off of U.S. assistance to the groups fighting the Soviet- and

Cuban-supported MPLA in Angola demonstrates the kind of domestic opposition that even intervention far short of war may incur. The War Powers Act of 1973 has the effect, arguably, of compelling presidents and military advisers to confine armed interventions to those actions that can clearly succeed in the 60 to 90 day period within which the president is authorized to initiate and conduct armed intervention. Nevertheless, every president must still regard a successful Soviet effort to undermine a friendly regime or establish an effective dependency hostile to U.S. interests as a threat to U.S. security with a significance that exceeds the intrinsic economic or geopolitical value of the country in question. Any president would be terribly vulnerable politically if a Soviet effort were to lead to an adverse change by armed force in the territorial-political status quo in the face of a U.S. political commitment or military assistance program. The credibility of U.S. will and power to protect U.S. interests against armed force and intimidation all over the world, and therefore international stability and order itself, might be at stake in such a situation. Furthermore, in the aftermath of Vietnam, Americans—as the opposition to "giving away" the Panama Canal demonstrated—are particularly sensitive about being pushed around and humiliated.

Given the spreading realization that the post-Vietnam international environment is anything but peaceful and stable and given the persistence of U.S. global interests and of the United States' broad definition of its security, the persistence of the view that military containment is obsolete in the Third World has depended largely on questionable new assumptions about the improbability of direct or indirect intervention by Soviet arms. But if confidence in the self-limiting quality of Soviet intentions continues to erode in response to events in Africa and elsewhere, then belief in the obsolescence of containment will have to rest heavily on confidence in local constraints on Soviet staying power, once positions of influence and dependency have been established.

Soviet reverses in Indonesia, Egypt, Sudan, Ghana, Guinea,

Mali, and Somalia—all positions of special influence reinforced with arms aid—have encouraged the hope that, even if Soviet military assistance succeeds in advancing the position of a client, the client will eventually turn against its benefactor. In this view, Soviet neocolonialism will inevitably run afoul of indigenous nationalism—the strongest political force throughout the Third World. But this view of the limits of Soviet influence in the Third World may turn out to be too optimistic. To an extent its validity depends on the ability of weak countries to resort to U.S. arms and money and other Western sources of support against excessive Soviet intrusions, but for political reasons this support may not be forthcoming in every case. For instance, in Africa the Soviets not only act with a greater semblance of political legitimacy than in Egypt, they combine arms shipments with military units that may be difficult for relatively weak political authorities to remove. Furthermore, the Soviet special relationship with Egypt lasted for fifteen years and is hardly a relationship that can be dismissed as ephemeral or insignificant.

A companion to the thesis of nationalist resistance to Soviet influence is the view that the weakness and volatility of African governments and the morass of conflicts among them will discourage or defeat foreign dominance. But whatever obstacles to dominance these conditions may pose, they certainly present the Soviet Union with tempting opportunities to play upon national, ethnic, and racial enmities, to provide armed support to insecure states, and to cultivate an international environment hostile to U.S. influence. Even if instability and chaos are not necessarily the objective of such Soviet influence, they may well be the result. The ensuing turmoil might, in turn, dangerously entangle both superpowers in ways that neither could predict nor would wish.

In any case, Soviet and Cuban moves in this field, fertile for the intervention of their arms and forces, have already shaken the early post-Vietnam assumption that the Soviet threat in the Third World died with the exaggerated fears of

wars of national liberation. The change of attitude is marked in
the Carter administration's oscillation between explicitly avoiding opposition to Soviet moves as the basis of U.S. African
policy and warning Moscow against violating the "rules of
détente."

The Spectrum of Limited Force

But what does all this mean for the relevance of U.S. limited-
war strategy in the Third World? It does not necessarily mean
that the United States or its European allies will or should find
renewed utility in fighting limited wars in the Third World.
Hopeful assumptions about the decline of the military threat to
vital Western interests in the former colonial areas of Asia and
Africa may not turn out to be valid. Nevertheless, the United
States' increased tolerance for disorder in the Third World
(manifest in its reluctance to intervene with its own forces or
even with arms assistance in local conflicts) may well reflect a
wise and enduring judgment about both the limits of U.S.
interests and influence and the efficacy of armed intervention
during a particularly tumultuous period of history. Certainly,
it is hard to imagine a less propitious political environment for
U.S. armed intervention than that which exists now in southern
Africa.

Moreover, the obstacles to U.S. participation in local wars
are likely to be reinforced by the growing Soviet capacity for
counterintervention and naval interposition in distant places,
by the acquisition on the part of less developed states of cheap
and easily operated modern weapons with great accuracy and
firepower,[9] by the high cost of fuel and supplies necessary to
sustain a large-scale military operation overseas, and by local
political restrictions on access to bases and passage through
narrow straits and territorial waters. The Third World has
become a particularly inhospitable, costly, and intractable arena
for great-power intervention in limited wars—at least for direct
intervention as opposed to support given to proxies.

Exactly how the multiplicity of actual and potential disruptions of international order may affect the vital interests of the United States and its allies, and whether these disruptions will warrant the limited use of Western military power is impossible to foresee. But the traditional response of military planners to this kind of uncertainty amid ominous instability and violence is to hedge their bets, to insure against unforeseeable, if not necessarily the worst imaginable, adversities. In this view common prudence calls for flexible military capabilities adapted to limited objectives under diverse political circumstances in a variety of contingencies that are not predictable. This is a sound strategy if the nation is actually willing and able to support it with the required forces. But such support depends, in part, on what kinds of limited-war contingencies the nation envisions. If one looks for clues in recent experience—discounting the exact replication of the past—a wide range of possibilities emerges.

The political and material impediments to the United States waging full-scale limited war as an instrument of policy in the Third World on the pattern of the Korean or Vietnam wars are immense, perhaps prohibitive. But these impediments do not necessarily obviate the utility of a variety of lesser forms of force. Indirectly—through arms transfers, military advisers, and in some cases combat personnel—the superpowers and their allies are already participating in a number of armed conflicts and potential conflicts throughout the nonindustrial areas. Military assistance is extended partly because it is one of the most effective ways to project influence and affect the local or regional configurations of power bearing upon the interests of the donors. Of course, military assistance programs, even when they align the United States and the Soviet Union on opposite sides in proxy wars, do not necessarily lead to direct intervention (indeed, they are often a surrogate). However, they are, in effect, the lower end of a spectrum of external armed intervention that extends through a range of kinds and degrees of armed conflicts up to large-scale protracted local war. From the standpoint of the superpowers such programs may play something of the role that insurgency and counterinsurgency were supposed to play in the 1960s.

Close to the lower end of the spectrum of potential interventions are quick armed strikes to protect citizens and property in foreign waters and territory. The fact that the most notable of these strikes—the U.S. rescue of the *Mayaguez* and its crew in 1977, Israel's rescue of terrorist hostages at Entebbe Airport in 1976, and the German rescue of hostages at Modgadishu in 1977—were successful and popular at home (and so, even, was the very costly and largely bungled Egyptian commando rescue in Cyprus in 1978) tends to legitimize sharply focused armed interventions for a variety of limited national and humanitarian purposes.

The brief and successful intervention of Moroccan troops, with French air transport, to thwart the advance of MPLA-supported Katangans in the Shaba province of Zaire in 1977 and the subsequent intervention of French legionnaires, backed by Belgian paratroopers and U.S. air transport, to rescue Europeans at Kolwezi who were trapped by the more effective assault of Katangans in Shaba in 1978, mark an ascending step, short of war, in the spectrum. The participation of thirty thousand or more Soviet-supported Cuban troops in African wars is a major extension of this category of direct intervention by small powers with the help of major powers. Although the magnitude of Cuban intervention is unique among non-African states, France bases some ten thousand troops in Africa to protect the anti-Communist "Francophone" states. And France, on the ground that it must play the role abandoned by the United States in preventing Soviet incursions, has already used these forces in Mauritania, Chad, and Djibouti. At the same time, Egypt and Saudi Arabia, charging that they are threatened by Soviet "encirclement" in the Horn of Africa, South Yemen, and Afghanistan, warily contemplate whatever forms of support (not necessarily excluding direct intervention) they can feasibly provide against Soviet-supported attacks across the boundaries of strategically important countries like Somalia.

In still a different category of small military encounters is the extended naval confrontation and glancing skirmish between Iceland and Great Britain in the so-called cod war over fishing jurisdiction. Whether this encounter foreshadows more serious wars arising from the expansion of offshore petroleum mining, fishing, shipping, and other uses of ocean resources will depend, in part, on how seriously small countries may damage the interests of major maritime states. The new issues of territorial jurisdiction, navigation rights, environmental protection, and resource exploitation in the oceans seem more likely to lead to armed clashes and wars between nonindustrial countries than between developed countries, or between developed and developing countries. Yet the great maritime states must prudently contemplate a variety of contingencies in which they might become involved in limited armed encounters at sea.[10]

Even the often-noted inhibitions that impede the major industrial states from using force against the nonindustrial states are contingent on the nonindustrial states not inflicting serious costs that can only be prevented or counteracted by military means. There must be a limit, moreover, to the extent to which nonindustrial states can resort to force in their relations with each other (and receive arms and even troops from the industrial states for that purpose) and still be immune from the use of force by industrial states to defend their own interests in the resulting chaos.

Recent examples of the limited use of force by major powers in the Third World only begin to illustrate the wide array of low-level military actions involving external powers that may be endemic to the Third World as the patterns of international power and interests grow more complex and diffuse and the sources and means of armed coercion multiply. In this kind of international environment one cannot rely on the constraints against participating in wars like those in Korea and Vietnam to exempt the United States and other Western countries from engaging in a variety of interpositions, naval encounters, block-

ades, police actions, raids, and skirmishes to support a variety
of purposes—from traditional interests, such as asserting territorial and resource rights, to possibly more novel objectives,
such as preventing genocide, preempting nuclear proliferation,
and blocking or pacifying a local conflagration. Nor can one
safely rely entirely on the military policies designed to cope
with the actual and hypothetical contingencies of the classic
period of the cold war to serve national policy in the more complex international environment that is emerging.

At the same time, the United States cannot neglect to plan
for more serious contingencies (like the wars in Vietnam and
Korea) in which intrinsically vital political and economic interests may be at stake in a local conflict and Soviet forces
may already be involved or poised to intervene. The Middle
East, with its concentration of oil supplies, its volatile internal
and external politics, and its accessibility to both Soviet and
U.S. influence and forces, is the prime example of an area in
which such contingencies may occur. There U.S. interests will
be more compelling than in Vietnam but the dangers of counterintervention and escalation will be more forbidding; hence, the
requirements for the politically discriminating use of force will
be even greater.

The Gap between Concept and Capability

Developing military-political doctrine for the expanded range
of contingencies outside the centers of industrial civilization
that the United States and its major allies must anticipate and
tailoring the training, organization, tactics, manpower policies,
and weapons systems of armed forces to cope with these contingencies are likely to be the most challenging tasks of limited-
war strategy in the 1980s. These tasks give a new dimension to
the concept of flexible and controlled response. The basic
rationale for executing the responses has convincingly survived
the vicissitudes of the last quarter century during which the
rationale was officially established, nurtured, and applied. But

the question that bedevils limited-war strategy now, as throughout the postwar period, is whether actual contingency and force plans and actual capabilities and operational doctrine to carry them out are commensurate with the demands that spring from the strategy of limited war and the conditions that might call for fighting a limited war. The difference is that now, more than at any time since the Korean war, this question arises from doubts about U.S. conceptions of vital interests and U.S. political will to support them.

Recognizing the variety of small or not-so-small wars that the United States may have to deter or fight in this turbulent period of international relations, the Carter administration has emphasized reliance upon conventional forces to protect U.S. global security interests. In its defense policies the administration sets the objective of dealing simultaneously with one major and one minor conventional contingency. It identifies the Middle East, the Persian Gulf, and Northeast Asia as areas where the most serious minor contingencies may occur; singles out the protection of oil supplies (by force if necessary) as a primary interest; and reasons that adequate preparation for "one-and-a-half wars"—a symbolic formula with which the Nixon administration, in recognition of the Sino-Soviet split, replaced the Kennedy administration's "two-and-a-half wars"— should be able to cope with brushfire wars and other lesser eventualities.[11]

Yet, actual defense plans and capabilities concentrate more than ever on deterring and fighting the hypothetical major war on the central front in Europe, and increased prepositioning of supplies in Europe reduces the flexibility of U.S. forces in meeting contingencies outside the area. A fourth of the army's active divisions are stationed in Germany. One division in Korea, scheduled to be withdrawn, may be kept there for awhile. Probably no more than two of the other divisions (located in the continental United States and Hawaii) can be spared for meeting Third World contingencies. Also, there are no signs that the U.S. penchant for overwhelming the adversary with advanced technology, massive firepower, and superior logistics—a penchant that reinforces the natural proclivity of the military to avoid intervention under current circumstances—has given way to operational plans for quick strikes and maneuvers that are better suited to likely Third World contingencies.

Nevertheless, let us concede the validity of the administration's claim that augmented quick-reaction forces not committed to NATO—three light marine and two army combat divisions; naval, amphibious lift, and tactical air forces; and mobile strike forces—will be adequate to cope with short and intense wars outside the NATO area. And, at the same time, let us assume that the defense budget and its allocation for service missions permit the creation and maintenance of such forces. The difficult questions remain: where, when, and how is the United States government prepared to use these forces, given the political inhibitions against Third-World interventions? Despite high official warnings against Soviet and Cuban interventions in Africa, and strong affirmations of U.S. determination to counter the recent growth of Soviet military power, the United States is not on the threshold of an assertion of U.S. power like that of the Kennedy period. Too much has changed. The general disposition to define U.S. security interests broadly and to express various degrees of anxiety over real and projected threats to these interests, especially where the projection of Soviet influence into new areas of contention is involved, is not accompanied by a commensurate disposition to contemplate the use of U.S. armed forces in peripheral areas. Therefore, if the Soviet Union exercises a modicum of discretion and avoids precipitating major crises while preserving the semblance of political legitimacy for its interventions, the U.S. reassertion of the concept of containment may be little more than rhetorical.

In this event, the gap between strategic concept and the operational power to support it could become greater than at any time since the Korean war. Diplomatic maneuvers, arms transfers, proxy wars, and the interventions of allied and friendly countries may help close the gap; but there will also be a danger that the historic pattern of an unanticipated threat, met by a belated, improvised, overwrought, and inappropriate U.S. reaction, will recur. One fact seems clear: the United States cannot turn again to increased reliance on nuclear weapons to close this gap.

Fundamentally, the gap now arises from the uncertainties of foreign policy, not from the ambiguities of military strategy. If the concept of containment that guided U.S. policy after the Korean war and reached its peak in the mid-1960s prevailed now, the United States—following the logic of limited-war doctrine—would be generating and projecting U.S. armed power even more energetically than during the Kennedy administration. But the United States, chastened by losing a war and conscious of the new complexities of coping with Soviet power, is caught between the lessons of Munich and Vietnam. Consequently, although the strategy of flexible and controlled response by conventional means is more widely accepted than ever, its utility as an instrument of policy where the prospect of local wars and Soviet intervention is greatest has never been more in question. Logically, the United States should either clearly devalue the nature and scope of its security interests to fit a drastic qualification of the original premises of containment, or else it should launch a major effort to attain limited-war forces capable of supporting the more demanding premises that still prevail. But this kind of logic, of course, is seldom the real basis of military policies.

6
Containment Revisited

The Record of Containment

An examination of the current state of limited-war strategy logically ends with speculation about the future of the foreign policy from which the strategy was derived. The core of this foreign policy was known as containment. Whether or not containment continues to be central to the core of U.S. foreign policy, limited-war strategy will be an essential part of U.S. military strategy as long as the United States has vital interests overseas that may have to be protected, ultimately, by armed force. But if containment is becoming obsolete or relevant only to a peripheral and diminishing aspect of U.S. foreign concerns, there will have to be a different answer to the critical question that now throws the role of limited war in the Third World into doubt—in what circumstances, if any, should the United States resort to limited war?

Throughout the cold war, U.S. government spokesmen went out of their way to avoid the word containment because of its negative and military connotations, but even the statesman who most outspokenly condemned the term—John Foster Dulles in the presidential campaign of 1952—was preoccupied with fulfilling the concept in practice. Not that containment was ever the whole of U.S. foreign policy, but it was the dominant element during the long period from 1947 to 1970 in which the principal U.S. security goal was to establish a reliable balance of power in Europe and the Mediterranean and to extend the deterrence of Communist expansion to Asia, the Middle East, and the Third World generally.

Containment was based on several key premises that became an operating consensus for leaders of U.S. foreign policy during the onset of the cold war:[1]

1. The Soviet Union relentlessly seeks to "fill every nook and cranny available to it in the world basin of power," in Kennan's words. This goal is based on historic and ideological factors that produce a deep anxiety about national security and a compulsion to uphold the regime's claim as the head of international communism.

2. Soviet leaders pursue the extension of power persistently, opportunistically, with ideological flexibility, and with caution, especially in avoiding a high risk of direct military encounters outside the sphere of Soviet army control.

3. Therefore, coexistence is not only essential, in order to avoid World War III, but is also feasible and compatible with the security of the free world if it is based on an equally patient and resourceful containment of Soviet expansionism.

4. Such containment requires opposing Soviet expansion by building situations of local strength and exerting counterpressure at constantly shifting geographical and political points.

5. Successful containment, in the long run, will lead to the moderation of Soviet expansionist tendencies, the normalization of Soviet international behavior, Soviet willingness to negotiate settlements of major conflicts of interest with the West on the basis of mutual accommodation, a loosening of Soviet ties with China and of Soviet control in its East European bloc, and perhaps even an alleviation of despotism inside the Soviet Union.

To a large extent these premises have been validated by the history of East-West relations, and containment has achieved its minimal objectives. Behind a shield of military containment, "situations of strength" have been constructed in Europe and

Asia where the United States could provide the "missing component" (both phrases are Dean Acheson's) of military and economic assistance. The Soviet Union has persistently tested the limits of Western resistance, particularly in Berlin, Korea, and Cuba, but has prudently refrained from pushing its aims at too great a risk of war with the United States. The Soviet sphere of control has been confined to the postwar boundaries controlled by the Soviet army. Even within these boundaries there has been a distinct erosion of Soviet hegemony in Eastern Europe, but the Sino-Soviet split—enabled, though not directly caused, by the containment of Soviet expansion—is the most striking manifestation of centrifugal tendencies in the Soviet sphere of influence. Finally, the series of East-West negotiations and agreements since the late 1960s on the inviolability of European frontiers, the security of Berlin, arms control, and principles of East-West relations marks the fulfillment of the ultimate political goal of containment. These negotiations and agreements give substance to the kind of détente that the authors of containment envisioned: the accommodation of conflicting interests within a stabilized relationship of competition and rivalry.

The success of containment, however, has not slowed the steady growth of Soviet military power or the projection of Soviet power and influence to weak and troubled areas of the Third World. Although détente—particularly, the rudimentary habit of mutual consultation on arms control, the avoidance of Berlin-type crises, and the habit of negotiating about specific sources of tension—has become a useful supplement to military deterrence and has made East-West competition more predictable and less nerve-racking, it has not basically altered the Soviet political system or its expansionist propensity. At the same time, détente has complicated the problem of maintaining a military balance by coupling it with the problem of orchestrating a global *modus vivendi* and by accelerating the loosening of alliances and the diffusion of power among states.

The East-West Equilibrium

The significance of containment in the changing international political environment needs to be assessed as part of an East-West equilibrium[2] —a balance between opposing forces—that has saved the world for over thirty years from an armed conflict between the United States, the Soviet Union, and their respective allies despite antagonisms that in prenuclear periods of history would have led to a general war. This equilibrium has become global in the sense that it has expanded to encompass almost every major geographical/political sector in the world and that a disturbance in one sector is increasingly likely to have repercussions in another. Stability in the central sector—the U.S.-USSR balance—is still the indispensable condition for avoiding world war, but stability at the center has never assured peace and order in the peripheral sectors. The proliferation of new nations, the maturing of their nationalism from romantic nation-building to incipient power politics, and their active assertion of separate and collective interests on the main international stage have thoroughly merged the problems of the industrial with those of the nonindustrial worlds. So the rising disorder in the periphery inevitably disturbs the center. As the periphery of the U.S.-Soviet relationship has expanded, the interactions between the central and peripheral sectors of the global equilibrium have become increasingly consequential, yet difficult to predict. It is in this context that we should view containment, along with détente, as a vital element—but only one element—of an increasingly comprehensive and complicated global equilibrium.

The present East-West equilibrium, it is widely recognized, has been growing more complex and fluid in recent years. This is because international politics are ever more multi-faceted and volatile. Power and diplomatic initiatives are more widely diffused among states. New regional powers emerge. The alliances of the superpowers are looser, less hegemonic. New patterns of conflict and alignment are developing. Local conflicts among new nations multiply and grow more intense. Resource and energy issues have come to the forefront of international politics. North-South issues cut across East-West issues, and the configurations of interests within both international political axes become more diversified.

In some ways these trends are more troublesome from the standpoint of developing coherent and effective foreign policies (and especially from the standpoint of coordinating allied policies) than the relatively polarized pattern of conflict and alignment in the classic period of the cold war—say, from 1947 to 1970—when the West was preoccupied with establishing an equilibrium in Europe and extending it to the periphery of Eurasia. The implementation of containment and the integration of containment with the rest of U.S. foreign policy have become commensurately more difficult.

In the more complicated structure of international relations that has been emerging in the last decade or so, the methods of containment have naturally become more diversified and harder to coordinate in terms of an overarching strategic concept. Arms control, arms aid, technological transfers, and trade relations are the newly elaborated instruments of policy, that, along with others, join the familiar military and diplomatic methods of building counterpoises and exerting constraints on Soviet power. The political objectives of containment, too, are broader. In many areas of the world, containment is not a matter of preventing the spread of Soviet influence or delineating spheres of influence. Rather, it depends on a variety of local and external constraints designed to moderate Soviet influence, often within countries and regions in which Soviet and U.S. influence coexist. Moreover, containment itself no longer defines as completely as it once did even the core of the Western industrial countries' foreign policies. Such definition is difficult in an era in which trade, monetary relations, oil and resource politics, and the demands of the nonindustrial and truly impoverished countries have attained the status of "high politics." In this international environment, East-West equilibrium does not depend as dominantly on a U.S.-USSR military balance as before, but must rest on several different kinds of equilibria in different geographical and substantive spheres of politics more or less linked to each other.

Nevertheless, the primary features of postwar international politics continue to shape our foreign concerns. The West's renewed anxiety about the growth of Soviet military power and about Soviet interventions in Africa, for example, shows that containment is still a central concern of the major democratic countries, a concern that affects almost all of their other foreign concerns. With the partial exception of the issue of access to Middle Eastern oil, the external interests that the United States and its major allies are most concerned to protect, with armed force if necessary, are directly or indirectly important largely because of Soviet influence. This circumstance will not be true forever, but it is evidently true for the foreseeable future.

Because of this overwhelming political reality, adverse changes in the East-West military balance are especially disturbing. The relationship between the military balance and Soviet policies and actions has never been a clear or simple correlation. Thus the USSR was most threatening to the West when, in the period from the Berlin blockade to the Cuban missile crisis, the West's military superiority was the greatest. The operational significance of Soviet military advances now, when the USSR has attained parity in the strategic sector, is still more obscure. With all the obscurities, however, the *trends* in the military balance are cause for deep concern.

In two major components of the balance—strategic nuclear striking power and both conventional and tactical nuclear capabilities in the European theater—the Soviet Union, having attained parity, continues to increase its relative power toward the achievement (if present trends continue) of a distinct superiority in the ability to fight wars of all types and magnitudes. In two other major components—the control and denial of global sealanes and the capacity to project and support forces overseas—the Soviet Union, although still inferior to the United

States and its allies, has attained a competitive position it completely lacked for more than two decades after World War II.

That the Soviets may credibly view their formidable drive for military power as compensation for military inferiority during years of the cold war, as an offset to geographical disadvantages and U.S. technical prowess, and as protection against the Chinese threat and the specter of a two-front war does not necessarily make the resulting trends in the military balance less disturbing. Yet the significance of these trends in real political terms is not obvious.

The military trends are most disturbing to many in the West who expected the Soviets to follow the Western logic of mutual restraint and stabilization of the military balance once they achieved a situation of rough parity. According to this logic, the Soviet persistence in amassing military power that exceeds the requirements of defense and stability in the face of Western limitation or reduction of military efforts portends offensive intentions. In reality, however, the Soviet military buildup does not clearly indicate how the Kremlin intends to use its power.

From the Soviet standpoint several factors warrant this buildup: the historic Russian fear of vulnerability, the determination to prevent the recurrence of the near-disaster of World War II, the compulsion to compete with the United States and its allies on a global scale, the emulation of what is seen as previous U.S. political exploitation of military superiority, and simply the conservative drive of the Soviet military for a safe but always indeterminate margin of security. Conscious of internal and external weaknesses in the USSR's ability to compete with a surrounding alliance of advanced industrial-technological powers, yet determined to consolidate the USSR's hard-won status as an ascendant global power, Soviet leaders and the military-industrial group that manages the economy need no special strategic or political justifications to concentrate the investment of resources on the one facet of national power in which the Soviet system excels. The proportion of that investment to the gross national product—now estimated at 11 to 13 percent—has scarcely varied. The West's military investments, in contrast, have fluctuated in response, alternately to sudden alarms of military gaps and crises and then to hopeful assumptions about the meaning of parity and détente.

On the other hand, the difficulty of inferring specific intentions from the Soviet acquisition of military power provides scant consolation if, as the evidence strongly suggests, the assumptions that initially underlay containment are still valid: that the Soviets strive ceaselessly and opportunistically to expand their influence and weaken all competitors. Soviet leaders can foresee no better than we the specific opportunities to achieve these general objectives. But the shift in the East-West military balance is nonetheless disturbing because of the persistent pattern of Soviet aggrandizement and the vulnerability of the changing international environment to Soviet opportunism. Therefore, common prudence warrants a concern that Soviet military power amassed for general reasons may enhance opportunities for specific kinds of troublemaking that no one can foresee.

The Balance Sheet of East-West Power

To assess the significance of the military balance or imbalance, then, we must turn to an assessment of the incentives and opportunities for Soviet restraint or troublemaking. These incentives and opportunities lie in the nature of the global East-West equilibrium, but the equilibrium must be appraised in larger than military terms.

In these larger terms a full balance sheet of the elements of power shows a number of Soviet weaknesses:

1. The Soviet economy suffers from serious structural constraints, which are rooted in the political system and cannot be completely overcome by Western trade and technology.
2. The USSR's relative economic isolation has deprived it of levers of influence in international economic institutions.

It is ill-prepared by economic capacity, technical know-how, or compassion—not to mention the Soviet conception of national interest—to sustain a genuine program of foreign economic growth as an enlightened instrument of policy and influence.

3. The Eastern European countries are restive and unreliable allies. The liberalizing tendencies in some of them potentially threaten the Soviet system itself, but Soviet repression might end what is left of Moscow's claim to represent a socialist commonwealth beyond the control of the Soviet army.

4. The emergence of China as an independent, not to mention hostile, power now bent upon modernization with the help of major adversaries to the West and East, comprising the world's foremost industrial powers, severely limits Soviet diplomatic and military options and distracts Soviet power.

5. The utter failure of the Soviet political system or ideology to attract foreign regimes and peoples and the Soviet inability to adapt to alien nationalities and customs restrict its foreign influence. These qualities, together with the suspicions aroused by its overbearing treatment of allies and clients, have been at the root of the USSR's expulsion from Egypt and other countries.

Not all these weaknesses, of course, are sources of Western strength. And the balance sheet of East-West power also includes some notable Western weaknesses: chronic domestic and international economic difficulties; dependence on oil imports at rising costs; conflicts of interest and policy between the United States and its allies on monetary relations, nuclear energy sales, and trade; a special vulnerability, by virtue of colonial history and the moral roots of Western civilization, to claims for economic, national, and racial justice organized by Third World countries; and, most markedly in the United States, the fragmentation of political power and the policymaking process as

the cold war consensus ceases to provide the integrating framework of a coherent foreign policy under presidential authority.

However, looking at the East-West equilibrium as a whole, one
is impressed by the constraints upon both of the superpowers—
constraints arising not primarily out of inherent weaknesses of
either but rather out of the many obstacles that the international environment imposes on the effective exercise of their
vast strength. The major source of these obstacles may still be
the superpowers' fear of each other; but, more and more,
they are also constrained by the sheer intractability of the international environment to the exercise of effective and enduring
control or influence. Many facets of the international climate
contribute: the instability of Third-World regimes; their enhanced assertiveness and impact on the international stage; the
increasing number and violence of interstate, ethnic, religious,
and other communal conflicts; the increased political inhibitions upon the use of force by the superpowers against smaller
states; the concomitant unreliability of proxies and clients; the
growing divergencies of interests and policies within the major
alliances; the more complex pattern of cross-cutting conflicts
and alignments among major states on a variety of trade, energy,
and resource issues. These types of factors greatly frustrate the
effective exercise of power by the United States and the Soviet
Union, although they fall short of producing the "impotence
of power" so widely noted by academic and journalistic observers. Consequently, although the geographical reach and magnitude of power have continued to increase for the superpowers—
if measured simply by the extent to which their actions or non-
actions affect other countries—their capacity to shape the
international environment—to control the effects of their power
on other countries in accordance with their interests and designs—has diminished.

Nevertheless, neither the United States nor the Soviet Union
can afford to assume that the intractability of the international
environment will automatically work to its advantage. The
Soviet Union, moreover, has an inherent advantage in that its
interests lie partly in exploiting local conflicts and the political

fragility of regimes in order to destroy the remnants of Western "imperial" influence. U.S. interests, however, generally lie in preventing sudden and violent changes in the territorial-political status quo—usually a far more difficult task. Furthermore, the Soviet Union has one component of power—military power, in terms of both its own armed forces and its capacity to arm others—that is growing relative to U.S. and allied strength not only materially but probably also in its political utility. Also, Soviet military power is relatively uninhibited by domestic constraints against its exploitation as an instrument of policy.

The West has distinct advantages of quite a different sort: the fundamental political and economic strength of the principal industrial democratic states; the material benefits they can offer other countries through economic and technological transfers and through trade and commerce; the basic appeal of governments that operate under the constraints and ideals of democratic processes; and their superior capacity for constructive diplomatic intervention, backed by economic incentives, to pacify the world's trouble spots. But the problem for the United States and its allies is how to use these advantages within a global East-West equilibrium to offset the Soviet Union's capacity to exploit Western weaknesses against the background of growing Soviet military strength. Obviously, this problem cannot be solved simply by building countervailing military power, but neither can building an adequate military base for containment be ignored in the search for a solution.

The first step in the solution is to get the Western house in order on energy, trade, monetary policies, and a host of other relationships in which allied cooperation can no longer be assumed to follow from common security interests alone. This is no small task, considering the divergencies of economic interests and the heavy intrusion of domestic concerns into all foreign relations.

It is also imperative to reduce the dependence of the democratic industrial giants on imported oil. Oil is not only a diminishing and increasingly expensive resource, but its price and supply are subject to the vicissitudes of political instability and manipulation. Reducing dependence requires the establishment now of extraordinarily far-sighted national energy policies within the Western industrial countries and an extraordinarily effective coordination of energy policies among them.

No less formidable is the task of coping in a reasonably coordinated way with a set of "transnational" problems that springs from competition for resources, environmental hazards, food shortages, population pressure, and the like, in addition to the regional and local problems that arise from national, ethnic, and racial conflict. All of these problems create international disorders quite independent of Soviet provocation, but coping with them is far easier to prescribe than perform. If it is possible to solve them at all, it will take a long time. The solution will depend on, among other things, the evolution of new and effective international institutions, laws, and rules of conduct.

Increasingly important to achieving a favorable East-West equilibrium will be shorter-term efforts to prevent and allay crises that create the opportunity for direct and indirect Soviet intervention. But the role of pacifier and mediator is an extremely delicate and sometimes risky one; and one cannot count on the Egyptian-Israeli diplomatic formula—which is difficult enough—to work under African or Southeast Asian conditions.

Closer to the core of East-West equilibrium are arms control agreements. Theoretically, they afford a cheaper, safer, and less provocative way of achieving a mutually acceptable military balance than competing arms production and deployment. In reality, they are not a substitute for vigilant defense programs. At best arms control agreements can somewhat limit and moderate arms competition and make it less unpredictable. At worst, they may impede measures of military security that can only be achieved unilaterally, and they may weaken allied cohesion.

In any case, arms control and other instruments of détente do not address the kind of disorder that now afflicts Africa, Asia, and the Middle East. There the United States can do little or nothing to stop the militarization of spreading national and communal conflicts. U.S. diplomacy is left with the fruitless task of seeking peaceful change in a revolutionary setting in which it lacks the political base for countering force with force. Yet without progress toward a modicum of order in the disturbed peripheries of the global equilibrium, the still rudimentary détente in the central sector of East-West relations is endangered.

In many parts of the world, however, the West can still utilize the direct diplomatic methods of containing Soviet expansion and mischief. Here it has certain advantages in exploiting the more complicated structure of international power. Thus the United States and, to some extent, its major allies naturally turn to linkage-leverage stratagems that exploit carrots and sticks in areas of economic and diplomatic strength to affect Soviet behavior in areas unrelated to East-West tension. For example, the West can try to make concessions on East-West commerce, science and technology exchanges, and the SALT agreement—all of which serve Soviet interests in détente—conditional on Soviet restraint in Africa and elsewhere. Or it can permit a deterioration of symbolic or substantive aspects of détente or further normalize relations with China and facilitate China's modernization in order to warn the Soviet Union against unfriendly maneuvers or to extract concessions in arms control and other areas of positive benefit. To an extent, such linkages are not only useful, they are the unavoidable consequence of a pattern of cross-cutting foreign interests and the force of public opinion at home. But as tools to be manipulated to produce precise results, they are blunt instruments, which carry risks of being self-defeating or uselessly provocative.

More appealing to the Western liberal imagination are ways of moderating Soviet behavior by engaging Moscow in the cooperative pursuit of convergent interests and encouraging it to play a responsible role in the international economic system. Nuclear nonproliferation, new laws of the sea, antiterrorism, and some environmental issues provide promising opportunities for East-

West cooperation. Despite the autarkic proclivities of the Soviet economy, Soviet economic connections with the rest of the world are growing more extensive and complex. Because problems like oil shortages and rising oil prices loom on the horizon, the USSR finds a stake in the orderly operation of the international economic system and in the acceptance of constraints on its freedom of action. Western nations can encourage this tendency if they harmonize their policies to this end and if, in return for Soviet respect for the rules of the game, they provide access to the much-needed assets and products of the West. It is utopian, however, to expect this cooperative approach to transcend or supplant the more competitive methods of moderating Soviet behavior, including military containment.

The Continuing Need for Containment

In the complex, changing, and uncertain East-West equilibrium of the 1970s and 1980s the West needs all the strategies it can manage to constrain the USSR. Indispensable to all of them, as at the onset of the cold war, is building and maintaining situations of local strength and stability and marshaling the kind of military power that will convince Soviet realists that military adventures and intimidation are unprofitable. It should be quite clear that the Soviet Union—for whatever combination of ideological, imperial, security, institutional, and just visceral reasons—will try to exploit its one conspicuous asset, the production and deployment of military power, "to fill every nook and cranny in the basin of world power." It should be clear that the USSR sees détente, not as the achievement of either stabilized parity of military power or lasting political harmony, but as a framework of relationships within which it can better pursue an advantageous balance of military power and exploit the most vulnerable areas of discontent and turbulence in the world.

Equally clear is that the United States is not going to abandon containment by choice, although it may undermine it by neglect or obsession. Whatever may be said (in theory) for models of foreign policy designed to escape the travails of containment through insulation from international disorder, devolution of power to allies, or the creation of new institutions and processes for international order, in practice the United States finds itself reemphasizing containment without the guidance of any grand vision of the future. Even while the relatively simple U.S. "empire" of the 1960s and 1970s disintegrates, the United States remains stuck with the role of being the principal and indispensable source of containment, whatever its larger mission may be.

Logically, reducing interests and commitments in order to bring policy into balance with diminished U.S. power to control the external environment may be the only feasible way for the United States to retreat from empire toward greater insulation from international disorder. Yet the United States would not readily give up status and influence even if it were willing to take the chance that its physical and economic security would not suffer.[3] Also, despite the hypothetical advantages of basing international equilibrium on an orderly devolution of military and diplomatic power from the United States to its major allies, the allies would be reluctant to take on the attendant economic and political burdens even if they believed that *their* security would not suffer.[4] Realistically, the United States can no longer rely on military and economic primacy to protect its global interests. But, in an increasingly heterogeneous and nationalistic environment, it also lacks the power to transform the international system in order to avoid the imperatives of traditional balance-of-power methods. "World order" is an enlightened model for the United States in its pursuit of transcendent goals. But the difficulty of developing rules of conduct, collective institutions, and modes of cooperation that can moderate the behavior of states and solve the dangers of interdependence is a process in comparison with which the problems of achieving previous U.S. missions of international order were elementary.[5]

Containment is not only necessary and unavoidable, but like

the models for escaping its travails, it is also feasible—not as an all-encompassing rationale but as one component of a complex global equilibrium. To be sure, many have feared that, in an international environment of détente and depolarization, containment would lose its domestic base of support, and the cohesion and strength of the West would collapse. There are grounds for this fear at the end of the 1970s when détente is substantive, as there were in the late 1950s when it was largely atmospheric. Yet the evidence of the last decade—for example, NATO's adoption in May 1977, of the Long-Term Defense Program to strengthen forward defense in Europe—indicates that Western governments and nations understand that containment and détente are two sides of the same coin—equilibrium. Even as that equilibrium grows more complex and fluid there is reason to believe that the Western powers can utilize their basic assets to offset the worst effects of ascendant Soviet military strength.

The Problem of When To Use Force

The biggest problem for the United States is not how to give containment material support or how to reconcile containment with the larger framework of U.S. policy, but when to implement containment with force. The critical problem, in particular, is how to translate containment into a strategy for using force by limited means and for limited ends to support various peripheral interests. These interests lie in areas where the expansion of Soviet influence by military means does not directly and imminently threaten the physical or economic security of the United States, its Latin American "sphere of influence," or its major allies but where nonresistance or ineffective resistance, through a chain of circumstances, may eventually have serious repercussions for vital U.S. interests. Of course, it is as difficult to predict and assess the repercussions of nonresistance as it is to compare the results of nonresistance with the costs of resistance. But, fundamentally, the problem of when to implement containment with force arises because of uncertainty about U.S. vital interests, including national security itself. This uncertainty must be understood not just as a reaction to Vietnam but as a result of the ambiguity of the conception of national security generally.

The core of national security is the survival of the nation-state—the preservation of its autonomy in internal and external affairs; but security has always meant more than survival, especially for great powers active in the mainstream of international politics. Security is a state of mind, not just an objective situation. It pertains to the degree of assurance or anxiety about national survival but, normally and more directly, about the external conditions upon which survival may ultimately depend. Therefore, it embraces what Arnold Wolfers called "milieu goals" that are thought to be necessary to assure survival: alliances, favorable balances of power, relative military capability, friendly states responsive to one's national interests, and ultimately something as general as a congenial international order.[6]

It is not only the subjective nature of security and its dependence on milieu goals that give the conception of national security its protean quality. It is also the broad and intangible character of the national self that is to be secured. The people of the nation personify the state and project upon it ideas of honor and prestige that become as much a part of their vicarious collective personality as are the nation's territory, allies, and vital interests. The national self, moreover, is a moral being— most markedly this is true in the United States—with principles and missions that give security a dimension that transcends pure self-interest.

It follows from the intangible and indefinite nature of national security and from its centrality among national interests that the motive of security is easily combined and confused with other motives. Where does the search for self-defense stop and the pursuit of primacy for primacy's sake take over? What is real security and what is merely a sublimation of self-assertion or aggrandizement? When does maintaining the credibility of the nation's will to use force for the sake of deterrence give way to the pursuit of national pride and prestige?

The expansive nature of national security, however, need not arise from motives more ambitious than self-defense. Paranoia is, in a sense, functional in the international system, where nations must seek their ends in a climate of anarchy. In order to play safe in this dangerous environment states normally attribute greater threats from adversaries than can be verified. It pays to be suspicious in a system that may heavily penalize those who assume the best, or even good, intentions on the part of adversaries.

Finally, the dynamics of international politics dictate that the importance of a threat to national security must be measured not only by the intrinsic value of the interests immediately threatened but also by the effects of the threat on the will of adversaries to challenge and resist each other in some future confrontation (and on the way other states gauge this will). Of course, dominoes do not always fall. Failure to thwart a determined adversary in one instance will not necessarily embolden or enable him to act with impunity in another. Yet no state can escape the psychology that invests an intrinsically small conflict with great significance if it is part of an overarching contest for stakes approaching survival. Moreover, when the nature of the contest and its weapons, like the bipolar and largely nuclear confrontation of the last thirty years, place a premium on deterrence, security becomes all the more dependent on intrinsically minor incidents that convey portentous messages about the will to use force.

The U.S. concept of security has always been active, outward-reaching, and somewhat missionary, even though oriented toward self-defense rather than aggrandizement. The concept expanded geographically and substantively from the time of the early achievement of continental security until World War II. It has expanded with the growing ability and incentive to pursue broader security goals as the magnitude and reach of U.S. power have increased. The cold war marks the most dramatic expansion. In the cold war the geographical extent of U.S. vital security interests became global. The intrinsic importance of particular countries to U.S. security was to a large extent—particularly, in the Third World—subordinated to the necessities of containment, which were regarded as virtually equivalent to the necessities of maintaining international order. The United States took on the responsibility of making the world safe from World War III.

After the Korean war it seemed that almost any point on earth that was believed to be threatened in any way by Communist aggression constituted a threat to U.S. security. And it followed that the United States would have to thwart such threats by one means or another, lest it encourage a chain of aggressions that could be stopped only at the unconscionable cost of another world war. By the same token, the protection of every country from Communist aggression became a test of U.S. prestige, upon which the credibility of deterrence and, hence, the preservation of international order depended. According to this outlook, a great range of U.S. interests abroad was absorbed into the concept of U.S. security. "National security policy," in common parlance, became equivalent to the management of all facets of U.S. power to contain international communism on a global scale.

It should be clear now that the U.S. concept of containment, and the concept of national security underlying it, became more sweeping and generalized than the United States' vital interests warranted, especially when applied to the use of force in the Third World. Consequently, in the service of containment, the doctrine of limited war not only exaggerated the efficacy and underestimated the costs of U.S. armed force, but also exaggerated U.S. security interests and the nature of the threat to them. If this truth was not learned thoroughly in Vietnam, it might have to be learned in Africa under even less advantageous political conditions.

What follows from this judgment is clear and simple in concept but unavoidably imprecise and complicated in practice:

the stakes warranting the use of force in peripheral areas should be more than national influence and prestige in the name of security. They should relate to specific milieu goals of substantial intrinsic value from the standpoint of U.S. military and economic security. Where Soviet forces, Soviet-armed forces, or Soviet proxies threaten such milieu goals, the importance of containing the threat with counterforce may be enhanced by the chain of consequences that might follow from U.S. abstention and Soviet success. But evaluating the importance of containment under such circumstances should be a matter of careful analysis, not an automatic inference drawn from historical analogies and doctrinal abstractions. Such an analysis should include a range of considerations that were either ignored or implicitly prejudged by U.S. foreign policy in Vietnam: Is there a prospect of a Soviet or Soviet-supported victory? What would be the political durability of such a victory? What would be the effect of such a victory on the regional or the global East-West balance? What would be the effects of victory on other potential targets of Soviet coercion or seduction, on U.S. allies, and on Soviet calculations about U.S. responses to future contingencies? And finally, is there a prospect of offsetting these effects by diplomatic measures, economic and political leverage, and other nonmilitary means? It should go without saying (but for our past propensity to neglect the point) that, along with the careful analysis of the probable consequences of nonresistance, there should be a scrupulous assessment of the feasibility and costs of direct versus indirect resistance. This assessment should include not only the critical factors in the military equation but also the political factors that received so little prior scrutiny in the Vietnam war: the political strength and cohesion of the recipient of U.S. assistance; the local, regional, and international political support of, or opposition to, such assistance; and the U.S. domestic political base of support or opposition.

Lest this process of reasoning be taken as a formula for paralysis, one must add that there can be no certainty about any of the considerations the process encompasses and that the opportune moment for effective action may pass if the decision whether to intervene with arms aid or with force must await anything approaching sure knowledge of the consequences. The function of any strategy is to order in advance a process of reasoning about the use of available means to achieve particular ends, not to short-circuit reasoning with conditioned reflexes or to overload reasoning with the search for certainty. The strategy of limited war has, perhaps, erred more in the direction of conditioned reflexes than in that of excessive caution; but the latter error could be as costly as the former if the incentives for Soviet intervention continue to rise. This is all the more reason to hope that U.S. statesmen, in drawing the balance between risk and caution, can rely on the kind of military capabilities that truly serve the broad range of interests which, for better or worse, still impose the preponderant burden of managing an East-West equilibrium on the United States.

Notes

Chapter 1

1. Mao's strategy, like all military strategies, was a projection and justification of the special circumstances—in this case, his experience in leading a rural revolution in China—in which particular political goals against a particular adversary were sought. Walter Laqueur examines the variety of theories and practices of modern guerrilla warfare in *Guerrilla* (Boston: Little, Brown, and Co., 1976).

2. Seymour J. Deitchman lists twelve "conventional" and sixteen "unconventional" wars in the period 1945-1962. *Limited War and American Defense Policy* (Cambridge, Mass.: M.I.T. Press, 1964), p. 27. I would classify at least two in the first category—the Congo and Yemen civil wars—as "internal."

3. The most important event triggering this development was the Soviet explosion of an atomic device in August 1949. This event, combined with the growing concern in some quarters of the government (especially the Policy Planning Staff of the State Department) about the gap between the United States' expanded overseas interests and commitments and the Soviet-Chinese threat to them, on the one hand, and inadequate U.S. and local conventional denial capabilities, on the other, led to a State-Defense team's report to President Truman called NSC-68 in April 1950. The central intention of NSC-68 was to alert the government to the magnitude of the Soviet threat and the military weakness of the United States and its allies to withstand it. The document did not stress the threat of limited wars or the need to prepare to fight them (although Charles Bohlen and George Kennan considered limited wars more relevant to U.S. military concerns than general war, which dominated military planning) but did argue that the growth of the USSR's nuclear capability required the build-up of U.S. and then allied conventional as well as nuclear capabilities to

cope with general and lesser wars. President Truman never explicitly approved NSC-68's recommendations, and budgetary constraints precluded acting on them; but although the study did not anticipate the Korean war, its rationale underlay the rearmament that followed. NSC-68 is reproduced in the *Naval War College Review* (May-June, 1975), pp. 51-108. See, also, Paul Y. Hammond, "NSC-68: Prologue to Rearmament," in Warner R. Schilling, Paul Y. Hammond, and Glenn H. Snyder, *Strategy, Politics, and Defense Budgets* (New York: Columbia University Press, 1962).

4. By 1960 the basic themes of limited-war strategy had been expounded by William W. Kaufmann (in 1954 and 1956), Bernard Brodie (1954, 1956, 1959), Basil H. Liddell Hart (1956, 1960), John C. Slessor (1954-58), Anthony Buzzard (1956), Denis Healey (1956), Raymond Aron (1956, 1959) in France, Paul Nitze (1956, 1957, 1958, 1960), Arnold Wolfers (1956), Maxwell D. Taylor (1956, 1959), Robert E. Osgood (1957), Henry A. Kissinger (1957), James E. King, Jr. (1957), Thomas C. Schelling (1957, 1959, 1960), James Gavin (1958), Glenn H. Snyder (1959, 1960), Alastair Buchan (1959, 1960), and Herman Kahn (1960). For a brief bibliographical essay on this period of limited-war writing, see Morton H. Halperin, *Limited War* (Cambridge, Mass.: Harvard Center for International Affairs, 1962).

5. The most influential exponent of the concept of limited war as a game-like manifestation of a general strategy of conflict was Thomas C. Schelling in *The Strategy of Conflict* (Cambridge: Harvard University Press, 1960) and *Arms and Influence* (New Haven: Yale University Press, 1966).

6. The most striking exposition of controlled escalation was Herman Kahn's *On Escalation: Metaphors and Scenarios* (New York: Praeger, 1965).

Chapter 2

1. Curiously, in their preoccupation with raising the nuclear threshold and distinguishing between conventional and nuclear weapons, western strategists ignored, and largely continue to ignore, the possible role of chemical weapons, if only as a counter to Soviet chemical warfare. While Soviet doctrine, training, and equipment reflect the view that chemical weapons are integral to military operations, the NATO countries have largely avoided the subject, partly on the assumption that even if the Soviet Union does not regard such weapons as part of tactical nuclear warfare, the United States must, pending the achievement of a comprehensive treaty to ban chemical warfare. Amoretta Hoeber and Joseph D. Douglas, Jr., "The Neglected Threat of Chemical Warfare," *International Security*, 3 (Summer, 1978), pp. 55-82.

2. See, for example, the argument for this strategic preference by Alain Enthoven, who was an influential systems analyst for Secretary of Defense McNamara. Alain C. Enthoven and K. Wayne Smith, *How Much Is Enough?* (New York: Harper & Row, 1971), chap. 4. Helmut Schmidt applied the U.S. case to German interests in *Defense or Retaliation: A Common View* (London: Praeger, 1962). For a notable contemporaneous criticism of this view on grounds of practicality, the dynamics of deterrence, and the cohesion of NATO, see Bernard Brodie, *Escalation and the Nuclear Option* (Princeton, N.J.: Princeton University Press, 1966).

3. Robert E. Osgood, *NATO: The Entangling Alliance* (Chicago: University of Chicago Press, 1962), chap. 5 ("NATO Goes Nuclear").

4. In *On Limiting Atomic War* (London: Royal Institute of International Affairs, 1956) and "Massive Retaliation and Graduated Deterrence," *World Politics*, 8 (January 1956), 228-37, Buzzard presented the case for distinguishing between tactical and strategic weapons within a strategy of "graduated deterrence" in order to make local defense effective. In his influential *Nuclear Weapons and Foreign Policy* (New York: Harper & Bros., 1957), especially chap. 6, Kissinger propounded a limited nuclear war strategy featuring special force structures, tactics and reciprocal restraints that would enable NATO to capitalize on its superior industrial and technological capacity without necessarily causing greater destruction than conventional war. By 1960, however, Kissinger had reappraised his views and joined the consensus that the United States should rely primarily on conventional war for local resistance, leaving tactical and strategic nuclear weapons as deterrents of last resort. "Limited War: Nuclear or Conventional—A Reappraisal," in Donald G. Brennan, ed., *Arms Control, Disarmament and National Security* (New York: George Braziller, Inc., 1961), pp. 138-52. Originally published in *Daedalus*, 89 (Fall, 1960), pp. 800-17.

5. Thus, according to U.S. officials involved in considering military contingencies at the time of the Berlin crisis, the U.S. government considered and rejected the resort to demonstrative uses of tactical nuclear weapons if conventional resistance were to fail in a local war, even though the United States enjoyed a considerable superiority in nuclear weapons at the time.

6. Colonel Richard G. Head elaborates these observations in a suggestive analysis of the contrasting Soviet and U.S. approaches to technology and strategic and doctrinal concepts: "Technology and the Military Balance," *Foreign Affairs*, 56 (April, 1978), pp. 544-63.

7. Robert Legvold, "Strategic 'Doctrine' and SALT: Soviet and American Views," *Survival*, 21 (January/February 1979), pp. 8-13.

8. Raoul Girardet, "Civil and Military Power in the Fourth Republic," in Samuel P. Huntington, ed., *Changing Patterns of Military Politics* (New

York: Free Press of Glencoe, Inc.), pp. 221-49.

9. Douglas S. Blaufarb examines the origins, development, and application of the U.S. strategy of counterinsurgency in the 1960s in *The
Counterinsurgency Era: U.S. Doctrine and Performance* (New York: The
Free Press, 1977). On the Kennedy administration's strategic concept,
see chap. 3.

10. Actually, the official rhetoric and popular impressions in the
1950s exaggerated the magnitude and equality of destructive power.
Notwithstanding the common parlance of "mutual suicide" and "annihilation" that came into usage following the dramatic H-bomb tests
and the popularization of Winston Churchill's phrase "the balance of
terror," until Soviet deployment of hardened and dispersed ICBMs in
the early 1960s the United States was probably able to knock out enough
Soviet strategic weapons on a first strike to restrict retaliatory damage to
considerably less than the level postulated during the Kennedy administration as "unacceptable" to the Soviet Union: one-fifth to one-fourth of
the nation's population and one-half of its industrial capacity. On the
other hand, Americans believed that the Soviet government would be
willing to tolerate a higher level of retaliatory damage than the U.S.
government could afford to risk.

11. See Klaus Knorr and Thornton Read, eds., *Limited Strategic War*
(New York: Praeger, 1962).

12. An authoritative commentary on this and other aspects of Mc-
Namara's strategy by one of his influential advisors and speechwriters,
William W. Kaufmann, is Kaufmann's *The McNamara Strategy* (New York:
Harper & Row, 1964). See, especially, pp. 92-95. McNamara's most
notable public statement of the strategy was his commencement address
at Ann Arbor, Michigan, June 16, 1962, reprinted in *The Department of
State Bulletin*, 47 (July 6, 1962), pp. 64-69.

13. Since the United States enjoyed a considerable margin of superiority in strategic nuclear striking power and had far more than enough
weapons for delivering unacceptable damage on a retaliatory strike, the
options for selective nuclear strikes were technically available; but the
targeting doctrine and plans, which were left to the Joint Chiefs of Staff,
were oriented toward massive strikes on both countervalue and counterforce targets.

14. On the Soviet compulsion to believe that victory is attainable even
in strategic nuclear war and the Soviet aversion to the U.S. conception of
limited nuclear options as intrawar bargaining measures, see Fritz W.
Ermarth, "Contrasts in American and Soviet Strategic Thought," *International Security* 3 (Fall, 1978), pp. 138-55.

Chapter 3

1. Failure and success are measured here by the achievement or non-achievement of the most limited objective of these wars: to establish the independence of the attacked country within its prewar boundaries at a political and material cost to the United States that was considered to be worth the objective.

2. The basic rationale was first spelled out in a National Security Council memorandum (NSC 124/2) endorsed by President Truman on June 25, 1952, which asserted that "the loss of any of the countries of Southeast Asia to Communist control as a consequence of overt or covert Chinese Communist aggression would have critical psychological, political and economic consequences." The loss of Southeast Asia "would render the U.S. position in the Pacific offshore islands precarious and would seriously jeopardize fundamental U.S. security interests in the Far East." It would force Japan's accommodation to communism. Therefore, since a Viet Minh victory against the French would jeopardize U.S. security, the United States must assure the French that it regarded their victory as "essential to the security of the free world, not only in the Far East but in the Middle East and Europe as well." *The Pentagon Papers: The Defense Department History of United States Decisionmaking on Vietnam*, Senator Gravel edition (Boston, 1971), vol. 1: 66, pp. 385-87. President Eisenhower explicitly likened the succession of threats that would follow from the loss of Indochina to Communist control to falling dominoes in his press conference of April 7, 1954.

3. The documents are voluminous, even in unclassified form. The experience of participants, recorded and recordable, is superabundant. There may soon be a flood of literature on Vietnam, but intensive monographs and comprehensive studies are still scarce. The military are just beginning to undertake the painful process of appraisal and self-appraisal. Among the few serious studies of the war based on more than personal experience and dealing with more than a particular incident or aspect, I found most useful Douglas S. Blaufarb, *The Counterinsurgency Era*, cited before; Guenter Lewy, *America in Vietnam* (New York: Oxford University Press, 1978); and Leslie H. Gelb with Richard K. Betts, *The Irony of Vietnam: The System Worked* (Washington, D.C.: The Brookings Institution, 1979).

4. These methods are perceptively described in Douglas Pike, *War, Peace, and the Vietcong* (Cambridge, Mass.: M.I.T. Press, 1969).

5. It does not follow, of course, that even the best prepared U.S. counterinsurgency forces could have successfully fought a war confined to the guerrilla level. NVA operations were an integral part of General

Giap's strategy, not just a response to U.S. main battle-units. In any case, such a war would have tied down great numbers of U.S. forces in static positions to protect the villages; and it is doubtful that the U.S. public would have been any more tolerant of the frustrations of large-scale guerrilla warfare than of search-and-destroy warfare.

6. The Nixon administration evidently believed that the Paris Agreements could be the basis of a free and self-sustaining South Vietnam if the United States would underwrite the peace with aid and sanctions. Essentially, the agreements prescribed the withdrawal of U.S. forces in return for the release of U.S. prisoners. They called for a cease-fire in place and free elections but permitted Hanoi's forces to stay in the South. President Nixon believed that the GVN could survive on this basis if Congress would continue to give it substantial amounts of economic and military aid and not oppose the president's threat to bomb North Vietnam if Hanoi violated the agreements. Actually, Congress banned future military intervention in Vietnam in 1974 and cut the administration's requested aid in half in 1975. Nixon also hoped that a strategy of dividing Moscow and Peking through détente with both would restrain Hanoi sufficiently to provide diplomatic support for a peace that could not be won militarily. But although this strategy did permit the United States to mine North Vietnamese harbors and destroy the railway links between North Vietnam and China without upsetting détente with Russia or the prospect of rapproachement with China, it did not induce Hanoi to accept a less favorable agreement than it was prepared to sign earlier, an agreement providing that the United States would withdraw while NVN troops remained in the South. Under these conditions Hanoi undoubtedly regarded the peace agreements as the basis for proceeding with the conquest of the South at a negligible risk of U.S. reintervention. It is quite unlikely that even the combination of U.S. aid and sanctions that Nixon desired could have prevented this conquest, given the imbalance of interests at stake between Hanoi and Washington and the weakness of the Thieu government.

7. On ROLLING THUNDER as an instrument of negotiation, see Allan E. Goodman, *The Lost Peace: America's Search for a Negotiated Settlement of the Vietnam War* (Stanford, California: Stanford University Press, 1978).

8. After President Johnson, in his San Antonio speech of September 1967, offered to stop the bombing of North Vietnam in return for peace talks and then unilaterally stopped attacks on the North (except against the continuing enemy buildup north of the Demilitarized Zone), Hanoi, in April 1968, announced readiness to talk with the United States about stopping all war acts so that peace talks could begin. It did so after insisting for three years that it would never agree to talks before the complete end of bombing. But this "concession" turned out to be more a tactical maneuver

to play on U.S. political will than a victory of controlled escalation. President Johnson followed Hanoi's agreement to talks by ordering the end of bombing north of the 19th parallel, although heavy bombing south of the parallel continued. In May the representatives of Hanoi and Washington began preliminary talks in Paris. But Washington was never able to achieve Hanoi's compliance with certain "understandings" of reciprocal restrictions on the war in the south, and the Paris peace talks became meaningless exercises in rhetoric until Washington agreed to withdraw U.S. forces from Vietnam while permitting Hanoi to keep its forces in the south.

9. Gelb with Betts, op. cit., chap. 9 ("Constraints").

10. About 34,000 Americans died in battle during the thirty-seven months of fighting in Korea; 46,500 died in Vietnam during 1961-1973. According to polls measuring approval or disapproval of these wars, approval fell off and disapproval increased much more precipitously in the Korean war until after the first fifteen months, whereas disapproval of the Vietnam war increased relatively steadily and did not reach Korea's peak of disapproval until May 1970. For the details see John E. Mueller, *War, Presidents, and Public Opinion* (New York: John Wiley and Sons, 1973). Of course, one cannot equate the two kinds of unpopularity exactly since the political purpose (and hence the morality) of the Korean war was never questioned, and its unpopularity sprang from the view that the war was not being prosecuted with sufficient determination to win.

11. In retrospect events in Southeast Asia may make the general objective of preserving international order against Vietnamese aggression and Soviet and Chinese intervention seem more creditable. By 1979 North Vietnam has already succeeded in dominating the immediate "dominoes" that were predicted to fall if South Vietnam fell: Laos and Cambodia. The defeat of South Vietnam and the withdrawal of U.S. forces, moreover, have contributed directly to the USSR's alliance with Vietnam and the PRC's support of Cambodia, its attack against Vietnam, and the resulting risk of a Sino-Soviet conflict, which could endanger vital U.S. diplomatic and security interests in East Asia and beyond. Even so, of course, this does not mean that the net political consequences of American intervention were worth the domestic and international costs the United States incurred. Nor does it mean that the United States would have gained the larger objectives of international order by persisting in the effort to save South Vietnam. What these events do indicate, however, is that the general objectives (or, in Arnold Wolfers' term, "milieu" goals) of balancing power and containing external intervention in potentially volatile areas of local conflict can have quite specific and significant, yet somewhat unpredictable, implications for U.S. interests and power which far transcend the intrinsic material stakes.

12. Potomac Associates, using polls on the mass public's view of the lessons of Vietnam, found that only 27 percent believed that the United States should not intervene in civil conflicts, even against Communists; 47 percent felt that the country should not have become directly involved in a land war in Asia; 34 percent felt that it should have used more force to win the war; 38 percent believed that the United States had no real security interest in Vietnam; and 30 percent attributed the defeat to the corruption and lack of fighting will in South Vietnam. William Watts and Lloyd Free, *State of the Nation III* (Lexington, Mass.: Lexington Books, 1978), pp. 122-23.

Chapter 4

1. Les Aspin documents the steadiness of the Soviet military buildup by fourteen different measures and notes that the U.S. defense effort, in comparison, has been erratic—a pattern most recently manifested in the decline of defense spending since 1968. "What Are the Russians Up To?" *International Security*, 3 (Summer, 1978), pp. 30-54.

2. By the end of the 1970s there was widespread agreement upon these rough generalizations about the U.S.-USSR military balance, though not about their political significance or policy implications. One should be aware, however, that even the most refined and sophisticated generalizations are incomplete and inconclusive. The reason is that there is no definitive method of taking into account all the factors that might affect the outcome of various kinds of clashes of U.S. and Soviet arms under various conditions. Static comparisons of the number and quality of arms in different categories are particularly unsatisfactory because U.S. and Soviet weapons systems are somewhat asymmetrical, serve different missions, and operate under different domestic and international constraints. On the other hand, estimating the dynamic interaction of forces in hypothetical wars has to include much guesswork, even for the military experts with access to war games and simulations. The most objective and useful unclassified analysis of the principal dimensions of the static and dynamic U.S.-USSR military balance as of the late 1970s is the Report to the Senate Armed Services Committee by John M. Collins, with a Net Assessment Appraisal by Anthony H. Cordesman, *Imbalance of Power: Shifting U.S.-Soviet Military Strengths* (San Rafael, Cal.: Presidio Press, 1978). It substantiates the generalizations above, but it also shows the considerable uncertainties and ambiguities in even the most refined military comparisons.

3. *Report of the Secretary of Defense to the Congress on the FY 1975 Defense Budget and FY 1975-1979 Defense Program* (Washington,

D.C.: U.S. Government Printing Office, March 4, 1974). The origins, content, and implications of Schlesinger's strategic initiative are examined in Lynn Etheridge Davis, *Limited Nuclear Options: Deterrence and the New American Doctrine,* Adelphi Paper 121, Winter, 1975-1976. The main features of a strategy of limited strategic nuclear options had been studied in the Nixon administration and formalized in NSDM 242.

4. Parity has come to mean, especially, a Soviet capacity to inflict damage upon the United States after being struck by U.S. strategic weapons that is no less devastating and "unacceptable" than the United States' capacity to do the same to the Soviet Union. But beyond this criterion some would add what Secretary of Defense Schlesinger called "essential equivalence" (and the appearance of essential equivalence) in overall striking power, including counterforce capabilities after delivering or receiving a first strike. In the first respect official U.S. estimates virtually granted the Soviet Union parity in the 1970s. In the second respect they anticipated parity by the 1980s. The controversial question at the end of the 1970s is whether the Soviets are achieving a militarily or politically significant superiority. Those who give an affirmative answer stress the greater throw-weight of Soviet missiles, which, with the coming addition of MIRVs and improvements in accuracy, could knock out a high proportion of vulnerable U.S. land-based missiles by the 1980s while reserving enough launchers to inflict unacceptable damage on the United States if it should retaliate with its bombers and submarine missiles. Those who deny Soviet achievement of a significant superiority stress America's present lead in targetable nuclear warheads, the superior accuracy and reliability of U.S. missiles, the superior throw-weight of U.S. bombers, and the deployment of 2000 to 3000 accurate airborne cruise missiles and a new MX land-based missile by the mid-1980s, in addition to the U.S. lead in invulnerable submarine-launched missiles, and the high absolute level of retaliatory destruction that U.S. submarines and bombers can inflict, beyond which comparative increments of destructive power are thought to have no meaning for deterrence or war-fighting. What no one can doubt is the great comparative growth in Soviet strategic striking power that began in the 1960s and continues. Experts dispute whether a SALT II agreement would retard or accentuate this trend, but virtually no one believes that the U.S. can, or even should try to, regain the superiority it enjoyed before the 1960s, either with or without an agreement.

5. One indication of limited expectations lies in reports of the Carter administration's comprehensive military study PRM-10. Although the study does not change the strategy of limited nuclear options, it is reported to conclude that in a limited counterforce nuclear strike, whichever side strikes first at land-based ICBMs will find itself significantly worse off than

the adversary in surviving numbers of missiles and missile warheads. Richard Burt, *New York Times*, January 6, 1978, p. 1. The same view is stated in Secretary of Defense Harold Brown's Annual Report for FY 1979: "None of this potential flexibility changes my view that a full-scale thermonuclear exchange would be an unprecedented disaster for the Soviet Union as well as for the United States. Nor is it at all clear that an initial use of nuclear weapons—however selectively they might be targeted—could be kept from escalating to a full-scale thermonuclear exchange, especially if command-control centers were brought under attack. The odds are high, whether the weapons were used against tactical or strategic targets, that control would be lost on both sides and the exchange would become unconstrained. Should such an escalation occur, it is certain that the resulting fatalities would run into the scores of millions." On the other hand, in a later discussion of defense programs the report states that strategic forces must be able not only to inflict unacceptable retaliatory damage on the Soviet Union but also to "implement a range of selective options to allow the National Command Authorities (NCA) the choice of other than a full-scale retaliatory strike if needed; and hold a secure force in reserve to ensure that the enemy will not be able to coerce the United States after a U.S. retaliatory strike," Department of Defense, *Annual Report, Fiscal Year 1979* (Washington, D.C.: Government Printing Office, February 2, 1978), pp. 53 and 105. The secretary elaborates these points in the name of a "countervailing strategy" in Department of Defense, *Annual Report, Fiscal Year 1980* (Washington, D.C.: Government Printing Office, January 25, 1979), pp. 75-79.

6. Among the most forceful and voluble critics was Herbert Scoville, Jr. See, for example, his "Flexible Madness?" *Foreign Policy*, 14 (Spring, 1974), pp. 164-77. An authoritative defender of the Schlesinger doctrine was Fred C. Iklé, Director of the Arms Control and Disarmament Agency, in "Can Nuclear Deterrence Last Out the Century?", *Foreign Affairs*, 51 (January 1973), pp. 267-85.

7. Benjamin S. Lambeth, "Selective Nuclear Operations and Soviet Strategy," in Johan J. Holst and Uwe Nerlich, *Beyond Nuclear Deterrence* (New York: Crane, Russak & Company, Inc., 1977). Fritz Ermarth, basically agreeing with this judgment, finds it plausible that Soviet contingency planning now includes limited nuclear options but believes that these options are intended not for bargaining and risk management but to economize on force, control its use, and provide for operational flexibility. "Contrasts in American and Soviet Strategic Thought," *International Security*, 3 (Fall, 1978), p. 149.

8. This argument is elaborated in Colin S. Gray, "The Strategic Forces Triad: End of the Road?" *Foreign Affairs*, vol. 56 (July 1958), pp. 771-89.

9. Comparing NATO and Warsaw Pact (WP) war-fighting capabilities is an extraordinarily complicated and tricky task, which leads experts to reach conflicting conclusions. But all experts agree that the Soviet Union has steadily increased the quantity and improved the quality of WP forces in every category, to give it major new strategic capabilities. Among the significant aspects of WP superiority in Europe are numbers of available combat troops and divisions, numbers of rapidly deployable reinforcements, armored mobility, and massed firepower for breakthroughs, antitank capability, air defense, battlefield communications and intelligence, the quantity and quality of TMW forces, including MRBMs and IRBMs, unity of command and standardization of forces. NATO's advantages in the quality of tanks and tactical aircraft are being rapidly overcome. In addition, NATO suffers from the geographical distance of the United States from the front line, the vulnerability of NATO ports and sea supply lines, the maldeployment of U.S. and other national forces in Europe, and the weakness of operational coordination among allied forces. Collins and Cordesman, *Imbalance of Power*, chap. 6.

10. This fear was publicized and substantiated in detail by the investigation and report of Senators Nunn and Bartlett. U.S. Congress, Senate, Committee on Armed Services, *NATO and the New Soviet Threat*, Report by Senator Sam Nunn and Senator Dewey F. Bartlett, 95th Congress, 1st Session (Washington, D.C.: U.S. Government Printing Office, 1977).

11. Several proponents of this strategy have written in *Orbis*: W. S. Bennett, R. R. Sandoval, and R. G. Shreffler, "A Credible Nuclear-Emphasis Defense for NATO," *Orbis*, 17 (Summer, 1973), 463-79; Samuel T. Cohen and William C. Lyons, "A Comparison of U.S.-Allied and Soviet Tactical Nuclear Force Capabilities and Policies," *Orbis*, 19 (Spring, 1975), 72-92; Marc E. Geneste, "The City Walls: A Credible Defense Doctrine of the West," *Orbis*, 19 (Summer, 1975), 477-90. See, also, Robert M. Lawrence, "On Tactical Nuclear War," Parts 1 and 2, *Revue Militaire generale* (January and February, 1971) pp. 46-59, 237-61.

12. Soviet strategic writing and pronouncements have recently acknowledged the need to be able to fight a theater nuclear war in addition to a small-unit conventional war or a general nuclear war, but they show virtually no recognition of the kind of limitations within such a theater war that U.S. strategists dwell upon. Rather, Soviet doctrine is oriented toward an offensive (or counteroffensive, in political terms) operation based on surprise, preemption, rapid territorial advance, and the employment of nuclear weapons at the earliest propitious moment, while relying on the nature of political objectives and the geographical restriction to limit the war. One can infer from this outlook that in a conventional war in central Europe the first sign of U.S. release of nuclear weapons would trigger

Soviet nuclear preemption and a full-scale effort to destroy NATO forces. On the Soviet approach to theater nuclear war see the chapters by William R. Van Cleave and John Erickson in Lawrence L. Whetten, ed., *The Future of Soviet Military Power* (New York: Crane, Russak & Company, Inc., 1976).

13. Congressman Les Aspin took this view in response to the alarming report of NATO's weakness by Senators Nunn and Bartlett in 1976. *Congressional Record*, February 7, 1977, pp. H911-14.

14. Secretary of Defense Harold Brown states in his Annual Report for FY 1979 that strengthening conventional forces must be given first priority in NATO's defense program. Balancing this priority with the imperative of nuclear retaliation, he declares, "President Carter has already made it clear that the United States does not rule out the use of nuclear weapons if the United States, its friends, or its forces are attacked. However, we continue to believe that we and our allies are best served by basing our collective security on a firm foundation of conventional military power. We cannot depend on tripwire theories or abstract calculations about cool and studied escalation. What we seek in conjunction with our allies is a major conventional capability sufficient to halt any conventional attack." *Annual Report, Fiscal Year 1979*, p. 79.

15. James Digby, *Precision-Guided Weapons*, Adelphi Papers 118, Summer 1975; Richard Burt, *New Weapons Technologies: Debate and Directions*, Adelphi Papers 126, Summer 1976.

16. The one example of the use of some PGMs (principally, antitank and antiaircraft weapons) was in the Yom Kippur War of 1973 between Egypt and Israel. Resulting assessments of the effects of PGMs have been inconclusive. Some early analyses rushed to the conclusion that PGMs provide a cheap and preclusive defense against blitzkriegs with modern tanks and aircraft. Subsequent analyses argued that this conclusion is erroneous because it overlooks decisive tactical factors. Jeffrey Record, "The October War: Burying the Blitzkrieg," *Military Review*, vol. 56 (April 1976), pp. 19-21. Uri Ra'anan, "The New Technologies and the Middle East: Lessons of the Yom Kippur War and Anticipated Developments," pp. 79-90 in Geoffrey Kemp, Robert L. Pfaltzgraff, Uri Ra'anan (eds.), *The Other Arms Race: New Technologies and Non-nuclear Conflict* (Lexington, Mass., 1975). Kenneth Hunt, "The Middle East Conflict 1973: The Military Lessons," *Survival*, vol. 16 (January/February 1974), pp. 4-7. In any case, differences of terrain, weather, geography, the deployment of troops and supplies, the composition and structure of total forces, etc. make doubtful the relevance of the Yom Kippur war to the effects of new weapons technology on war in Europe.

17. The problem that long-range cruise missiles pose for arms control

agreements lies not only in the difficulty of verifying limitations but also in that they break down the distinction between strategic and tactical (or theater) weapons, which underlies both SALT and MBFR. This distinction, however, is also threatened by other weapons, including NATO's "forward based system" ("tactical" aircraft based in Europe and on aircraft carriers) and Soviet MRBMs (particularly the SS-20), with flight ranges that reach between NATO territory and the Soviet Union.

18. On the advantages and disadvantages of mini-nukes from the standpoint of defense and deterrence in Europe, see Laurence W. Martin, "Flexibility in Tactical Nuclear Responses," Holst and Nerlich, *Beyond Nuclear Deterrence*. Particularly unfortunate in its effects on deterrence and allied confidence in U.S. nuclear protection would be a strategy that tied mini-nukes not only to the early first-use of nuclear weapons but also to the geographical restriction of their use to NATO territory in order to enhance the prospect of reciprocal limitation of local nuclear war.

19. Alain C. Enthoven presents this argument in "U.S. Forces in Europe: How Many? Doing What? ," *Foreign Affairs*, vol. 53 (April 1975), pp. 513-32.

20. Steven Canby and Robert W. Komer are foremost among those arguing for almost a decade for the restructuring of NATO's forces in order to get more fighting power out of manpower on the model of the Soviet Union's smaller divisions. See, for example, Canby, "NATO Muscle: More Shadow than Substance," *Foreign Policy*, no. 8 (Fall, 1972), and Komer, "Treating NATO's Self-Inflicted Wound," *Foreign Policy*, no. 13 (Winter, 1973-74). Neither sees standardization as a panacea. See also, Richard D. Lawrence and Jeffrey Record, *U.S. Force Structure in NATO: An Alternative* (Washington, D.C.: The Brookings Institution, 1974).

21. Uwe Nerlich, "Continuity and Change: The Political Context of Western Europe's Defense," and Henry S. Rowen and Albert Wohlstetter, "Varying Response with Circumstance," in Holst and Nerlich, *Beyond Nuclear Deterrence*.

Chapter 5

1. Mass public opinion poll data suggest that whereas U.S. willingness to come to the aid of an ally or firm friend that is invaded by a Communist country, as in the Korean war, has increased significantly since 1974, public willingness to intervene against a more generalized or indirect Communist threat still reflects the decline induced by the reaction to Vietnam. John E. Muller, "Changes in American Public Attitudes Toward International Involvement," in Ellen P. Stern, ed., *The Limits of Military Intervention* (Beverly Hills, Calif.: Sage Publications, 1977). Summarizing

recent studies of public attitudes, Daniel Yankelovich concludes that "the chief impact of the war [in Vietnam] has been to make Americans more selective and wary of military entanglements where U.S. security interests are not believed to be critically involved." Yankelovich, "Cautious Internationalism: A Changing Mood Toward U.S. Foreign Policy," *Public Opinion*, 1 (March/April 1978), pp. 12-16. A similar conclusion was reached by Potomac Associates in 1976, which also showed a distinct trend in favor of coming to the defense of allies, retaining U.S. preeminence in power, and supporting defense expenditures, as compared to 1974. Walter Slocombe, et. al., *The Pursuit of National Security: Defense and the Military Balance* (Washington, D.C.: Potomac Associates, 1976).

2. "The survival of revolutionary rule remains the foremost objective of their foreign policy." Jorge I. Dominguez, "Cuban Foreign Policy." *Foreign Affairs*, vol. 51 (Fall 1978), p. 84.

3. In Angola and Ethiopia the USSR demonstrated the growth of "projection" power in the last decade or so by transporting to these overseas areas decisive quantities of heavy and light arms and thousands of Cuban troops and, during the Angolan intervention, deploying significant naval formations in the area. This feat is in striking contrast to the Soviet inability to fly in more than a few trucks and transport aircraft to help Lumumba's forces in the Congo crisis of 1960-1961. Nevertheless, except in adjacent land areas, the Soviet capacity to project forces does not nearly equal the U.S. capacity. Although Soviet naval capacity to deny the United States unimpeded use of the sealanes has increased dramatically since the mid-1960s and Admiral Gorshkov has persistently promoted the Soviet navy's mission of protecting "national liberation movements," Soviet naval forces are no match for U.S. forces in supporting countries or factions in local wars overseas. Consequently, the practical effect of enhanced Soviet overseas intervention capabilities depends on whether these capabilities are likely to encounter opposition from U.S. forces.

4. Congressional Research Service, Report to Committee on International Relations, House of Representatives, *The Soviet Union and the Third World: A Watershed in Great Power Policy?*, 95th Congress, 1st session, 1977.

5. Donald S. Zagoria believes that another new element in Soviet Third-World policy is a strategy to establish a new alliance system in Africa and Asia based on support to Marxist-Leninist parties that gain state power— "a looser eastern version of the Warsaw Pact." "Into the Breach: New Soviet Alliances in the Third World," *Foreign Affairs*, 57 (Spring, 1979), p. 738.

6. As Chester A. Crocker observes, "Africa is one of the few regions in which political-military instruments—gunboat diplomacy, arms transfers,

military and security-related training and advisors, logistics experts, intelligence operatives, and combat support—are easily used by an outside power. So far, the Soviet 'comparative advantage' in these fields of activity can be brought to bear without either (a) provoking a substantial Western response or (b) drawing attention to Moscow's meagre capacity to provide other (non-military) forms of support and assitance." Mimeographed copy of testimony submitted at the request of the Senate Foreign Relations Committee, October 23, 1978, p. 3.

7. Robert Legvold examines the variety of interests and aims that may motivate Soviet behavior in Africa in chap. 5 ("The Soviet Union's Strategic Stake in Africa") of Jennifer Seymour Whitaker, ed., *Africa and the United States* (New York: New York University Press, 1978).

8. Confirmation of this imperative came in March 1979, when President Carter, largely in response to Saudi anxieties, authorized on an emergency basis and without seeking congressional approval the transfer of heavy arms to North Yemen in order to stop an invasion by South Yemen forces that were supplied, trained, and organized by the USSR.

9. The utility of PGMs to small countries defending themselves against major powers is a controversial subject, turning on a number of characteristics of these weapons, such as their cost, the difficulty of training troops to use them, the sophistication of command and control systems, and the effectiveness of countermeasures, not to mention the factors of terrain and weather that affect the utility of PGMs anywhere. The current consensus, however, is that PGMs are, on balance, attractive defensive weapons for smaller countries, particularly as compared to the high-performance, high-cost weapon systems such countries have been buying. See, for example, Anne Hessing Cahn and Joseph Kruzel, *Controlling Future Arms Trade* (New York: McGraw-Hill, 1977), pp. 52-62.

10. Robert E. Osgood, "Military Implications of the Law of the Sea," in *Power at Sea: Part I: The New Environment*, Adelphi Papers 122, Spring, 1976. Barry Buzan examines the numerous sources of dispute arising from uses of the oceans and from the effort to form a new regime to order these uses and concludes that, although very few such disputes are likely to lead to serious military conflicts, many will result in low-level conflicts and exacerbate other kinds of disputes. *A Sea of Trouble?: Sources of Dispute in the New Ocean Regime*, Adelphi Papers 143, Spring, 1978.

11. According to Secretary of Defense Harold Brown, "As has been the case since 1969, we want sufficient nonnuclear forces so that, in conjunction with allies, we can deal simultaneously with one major contingency (of the magnitude that could arise in Central Europe) and one lesser contingency (of the magnitude that could occur, for example, in the vicinity

of the Persian Gulf). If, with our current and programmed capabilities—
and with our allies—we can manage two such contingencies, we consider
nonnuclear deterrence of attacks on our interests reasonably well assured."
Department of Defense, *Annual Report, Fiscal Year 1980* (Washington,
D.C.: U.S. Government Printing Office, January 25, 1979), p. 100.

Chapter 6

1. These premises are distilled from the contemporaneous statements,
publicly and within the government, by George F. Kennan, Dean Acheson,
and a number of others. There were, of course, differences among them
and, particularly in the case of Kennan's published statements, ambiguities
that led to different interpretations. On Kennan's conception of containment and the disputed role of "counterforce" in his published statement,
see George F. Kennan, *Memoirs: 1925-1950* (Boston: Little, Brown, 1967),
chap. 15 ("The X-Article"), and John Lewis Gaddis, "Containment: A
Reassessment," *Foreign Affairs*, 55 (July 1977), pp. 873-87.

2. "East" and "West" are used here as political, as much as geographical, terms. By "East" I mean the Soviet Union and its European allies. By
"West" I mean primarily the United States, its European allies, and Japan.

3. The case for greater insulation by reducing interests and commitments, despite the acknowledged costs in stimulating international disorder, is best argued by Robert W. Tucker, *A New Isolationism: Threat or
Promise?* (New York: Universe Press, 1972), and Earl C. Ravenal, "Soviet
Strength and U.S. Purpose," *Foreign Policy*, 23 (Summer, 1976), 51, and
"Consequences of the End Game in Vietnam," *Foreign Affairs*, 53 (July,
1975), pp. 651-67.

4. I have presented the case for and against such devolution in Robert
E. Osgood and others, *Retreat from Empire?: The First Nixon Adminis-
tration* (vol. 2 of *America and the World*), chap. 6 ("The Diplomacy of
Allied Relations: Europe and Japan"). See, also, Michel Tatu, "The
Devolution of Power: A Dream?" *Foreign Affairs*, 53 (July 1975),
pp. 668-82.

5. Stanley Hoffmann ably argues the case for the United States adopt-
ing a policy of "world order" and thoroughly considers the obstacles to
the success of such a policy in *Primacy or World Order: American Foreign
Policy Since the Cold War* (New York: McGraw-Hill Book Co., 1978).

6. Arnold Wolfers, *Discord and Collaboration* (Baltimore: The Johns
Hopkins Press, 1962), chap. 5 ("The Goals of Foreign Policy").